A View from My Window

❦

REAL STORIES
for REAL WOMEN

BY SYLVIA FORREST

CONTENTS

Grandmothers

INTRODUCTION

Introduction

Pour a cup of coffee, make yourself comfortable, and I'll introduce you to some of my favorite women. These women are young, old, single, married, and divorced. Some are very wise, while others still have a lot to learn. All of them have had an impact on my life. I'm grateful for having known each one of them, and hope that you will enjoy meeting them as they are presented. Throughout the book, you will also get a glimpse of a younger me who is insecure, makes mistakes, and awkwardly dances around the boundary between childhood and adulthood.

Please forgive the occasional intrusion of some people I have never met, particularly Jane Austen and Oscar Wilde. Ms. Austen is my patron saint. Whenever I need to relax, I open to a random page of *Pride and Prejudice*, and my troubles fade to nothing. I am more familiar and at home with her world than I am with my own, and hope you find her words as timeless as I do. As for Mr. Wilde, he was a brilliant satirist who just plain cracks me up. Every once in a while, he throws us off-balance by saying something poignant. I love that.

This book is divided into three sections. We start with young women stumbling along the path to independence.

Some of them demonstrate incredible bravery, and strike out on their own. Others find smaller ways to assert themselves, or fail and suffer the consequences. Relationships fall apart, and roses bloom in the ashes for those who are brave enough to lift the watering can. We also cannot avoid taking notice of some questionable judgments. In one story, I am blamed for not saving a friend from a bad decision; in another, my husband stops me from making one, myself. It is a humbling contrast that I put forward without shame, knowing that we all learn from our mistakes, hoping I will be wiser the next time, and unsure of whether I would change what I did if I could.

Next we take a look at motherhood, that incredible vocation that threatens to undo some of the ego-building and self-awareness we achieve in early adulthood. Now, we must place others' needs above our own, and find a sense of balance, lest we lose ourselves completely. These stories include the astonishing love mothers feel, and the hopes and fears that come with it. Many of these stories are about me, mostly because I'd rather expose my own weaknesses than venture to guess at those of the women around me. That would be judgmental, and Heaven knows, I wouldn't want to be judged by them. We, all of us, live in glass houses. We all do the best we can with what we have.

As for the third and final section, it may seem that I have idealized my grandmothers; so be it! We should all be remembered for the good we leave behind, in memories and lessons for younger generations. After writing her stories, for instance, I learned that my grandmother Sadie's relationship with her sister had been volatile from beginning to end. Sadie never spoke of this. I refuse to "correct" what I wrote because of the "facts." The lessons she always taught me included acceptance and forgiveness, and the value of these lessons far outweigh "truth." There are always multiple truths, especially when telling other people's stories. If necessary, let Heaven sort through them. I'm staying out of it.

So! Here we are, ready to begin. I've got my coffee ready. Do you?

WOMANHOOD

WOMANHOOD

When my college friend, Tess, first spent the night with her boyfriend, she told me, "Now I know what it means to be a woman!" I listened to her declarations of love, the thrill of leaving behind her girlhood for something much better. I noticed the glow in her eyes, the quiver in her voice, the teddy bear on her bed, and the box of Little Debbie treats on her dresser. It didn't take a genius to figure out that Tess was both girl and young woman, and no amount of sex was going to catapult her into adulthood.

When does a girl become a woman? I think it happens gradually, as she learns to make choices for herself and to accept the consequences of those decisions. It happens as she stumbles, falls, and picks herself up again. It happens as she learns to differentiate herself from the rest of the world, and hopefully to like herself the way she is. Even after I married, bought my first home, and bore my first child, I still felt more like a girl than a woman.

More than men do, women share and grow as a collective. Women often seek their friends' opinions, though they may ignore them to do as they choose, anyway. Other times, they ignore their own instincts and go wildly off track in order to follow the advice of the collective. I have made some questionable decisions and have written about them without shame. Some of my friends have also faltered. While I have protected their privacy and identities in this book, I do not think less of them because they are not perfect. We should celebrate the mistakes that we commit and learn from them, because we do not need to make those mistakes again. My wish is that you, gentle reader, will be able to learn from some of these stories and avoid falling into the traps in which my friends and I have fallen.

Women give advice, cry on each other's shoulders, and help each other in many ways without expecting anything in return. I have been blessed to know many strong, loving women, and have often marveled that they have sought my friendship—these vibrant women who have accomplished so much! I have friends who are doctors, nurses, writers, lawyers, managers, publicists, artists, teachers, and consultants. Many of these women simultaneously hold these jobs, raise children, adopt children, travel, play tennis, volunteer, scrapbook, run marathons, earn graduate degrees, and negotiate peace in the Middle East. OK, that last one is an exaggeration. As for me? I have no exciting career, hobbies, travel stories, or positions on boards of charities. What do they see in me? Should I try to be more like them?

After my business school graduation, a large corporation hired me for their operations unit. An opening came available, soon after, to work on a project with Janet, a corporate star who had been there for years. Janet could have taught me a great deal. She was brilliant, polished, articulate, and very well-respected at the company. My grad school classmates would have killed to get an assignment like that. I turned it down. Why? The project required up to 50 percent travel, and my son Andrew was barely two-years-old. I couldn't leave him. There would be enough other project work to keep me busy, or so I thought.

In less than a year, the project work had dwindled to nothing. Soon I had no more than two hours' work every day. I begged my manager for an assignment, even asked whether I could help the division secretary prepare for end-of-quarter. I think the company was simply waiting for me to quit, but my salary was too substantial to walk out on. I began perusing the Help Wanted section, even at my desk during business hours. The items I circled did not reflect my chosen career path. I saw ads for publishing assistant, editorial assistant, and educators—jobs that offered one-third my current compensation, and for which I was woefully unqualified. On top of it all, I was pregnant with our second child, and beginning to show. Who would hire me?

Providence did me a favor. Before I suffered a complete mental breakdown, my husband David decided to move us to Kentucky, or that's one version of the story. Here's another: David's father suffered a heart attack, and David flew out to be with him. He asked David to consider moving home to be near him, and David agreed to discuss it with me. I had packed up half the house before he'd even boarded his return flight. Who cares how it happened? It did! I would be free of my gilded cage!

We moved to Kentucky, and I became a full-time mother. Life was sweeter than I knew it could be. I didn't realize until years later how much extra pressure I'd put on David when I stepped out of the workforce. It didn't occur to me that it might have been a selfish decision, and that I should have at least discussed it with him. I had decided we would move, and I decided to become a full-time housewife. It felt so good to want something that felt right, after years of doing things that felt wrong. I am lucky to have such an understanding and generous husband. While I am not proud of my behavior, I will tell you that other than marrying, it was the first time I truly felt like a grown-up. I had made a choice on my own, for something I really wanted.

I kept in touch via email with friends from my corporate life. One day I received a surprising letter from Janet: she had decided to ask the company for a part-time position, and thanked me for helping her put work into perspective. She admired me for having the courage to leave the workforce, envied the extra time I would have with my children, and wished she hadn't waited as long as she had to try to balance her life. I had been her inspiration. The woman I'd always wished to be more like, actually wanted to be more like me!

We never know who will provide us with inspiration, or whether those who inspire us are worthy of admiration. I certainly didn't deserve any. I can only conclude that the world is truly a crazy place.

In the pages that follow, you will find stories of small victories, big mistakes, and unanswered questions. These pages tell stories of relationships that survived, and relationships that failed. We all experience things like these on our path from girlhood to adulthood. In my case, the path began with a trilogy of events: college graduation, my first apartment, and my discovery of flavored creamers. Enjoy.

Carpets and Coffee

When a girl leaves her family home, she has an almost magical, liberating opportunity to express her individuality in her physical surroundings. Some women are blessed with creative talents or visions that help the process along. My friend Thalia, graphics designer, faux-painted her grandmother's dining room set. Sharon, publications artist, sewed her own curtains. Kim, romantic English major with formidable student debt, combed thrift stores to create a "shabby chic" look, years before it had become a trend.

Even if I'd discovered my "inner decorator" (which I hadn't), I would have to find other ways to express myself. For my first post-college living experience, I was going to share a condo owned and decorated by one of my mother's acquaintances, and already inhabited by her daughter, April. I moved in eagerly, lugging two suitcases full of office-appropriate attire with the tags still on. The apartment was in a tall, modern building with reserved parking places, two elevators, and laundry on every floor. I'd hit the jackpot! In addition, I acquired a mentor: at twenty-four years of age, April exhibited more style and sophistication than I had ever dreamed of achieving. She would be a living, breathing model to which I could aspire.

In short order I learned there is an art to living with other people, and more precisely, with people who know your mother. If I had complaints, I couldn't share them with Mom; she would defend her friend's daughter and remind me how grateful I should be for the apartment. I tried to impress April so she'd say nice things about me to her mother, who would then hopefully pass them onto my mother. Life became a dance on tiptoes. Actually, life soon became a dance on top of furniture.

April's apartment had brand-new carpeting. Oh, how she loved the thick, white, short-weave plush! We removed our shoes upon entering and were careful not to eat in the living room or anywhere outside the kitchen, lest crumbs fall from our lips onto the pristine, beloved, wall-to-wall carpet. In fact on movie nights, we took the TV out of the wall unit and heaved it onto the coffee table so that we could sit at the kitchen counter with our popcorn. Twice a week, April vacuumed the apartment. She loved the look of the even tracks she made with her Hoover, like a professional ballfield with perfectly symmetrical stripes of this-way and that-way mowing. When she was finished, April would stand on the furniture, lift the Hoover and place it onto the tiled floor of the entryway. Then she would curl up on the sofa and admire her work.

On my very first Tuesday night—a vacuum night—I walked sock-footed towards the kitchen to find something for dinner. "Aaaaaa! Get off!" April screamed. In a panic, I raced to the kitchen and checked the bottoms of my socks for wet paint. I felt a mix of relief and confusion as I saw nothing there. Cautiously and curiously, I peered over the breakfast bar to where April was perched on the white sofa.

"Don't do that again!" she cried.

I looked around. "Um...are you talking to me?"

"Yes, of course!" She looked exasperated. "I mean, I just vacuumed! Duh!"

So twice a week I stayed on my bed for an hour, waiting to be given permission to step towards the kitchen for dinner. I'd hear the Hoover running, the *thunk* of the vacuum onto the tile entryway. Finally, the closet door would open, which meant that April had enjoyed the view of the carpet enough for the night and had walked across it to put the vacuum cleaner away. Then it was time for broiled chicken.

We always ate broiled chicken on vacuum nights. Thin as a rail, April had unusual opinions on nutrition: broiled chicken on vacuum nights, extra-large butter pecan milkshakes for brunch on weekends. For the calcium. So, OK, she was cooking for both of us and I couldn't complain. I chewed (and chewed, and chewed, and chewed) on the dry, tasteless chicken twice a week until it was time to move out. But here's the good part: her tyranny did not apply to my coffee.

April was an early-to-riser. She set the automatic coffee maker the night before, and left me a cup or two when she went to work. She always left a note on the counter: "Please be sure you take everything apart and wash by hand in hot, soapy water. Towel dry and put away. "

I started drinking coffee in college because I thought it was a grown-up thing to do. Black was pretty hard to take, so I added some sugar. Then some cream. Before long, I'd grown addicted to coffee that looked and tasted more like hot cocoa. April's refrigerator had never known cream before I moved in. It felt wonderfully rebellious to buy the cream and put it on the shelf next to the nonfat sour cream and fat-free butter-substitute in the refrigerator that was carefully organized by food group. A month later, I bought a larger container. This now reeked of rebellion, as the larger cream did not fit on the shelf; it had to be put in the door of the fridge, with the beverages. Cream did not count as a beverage. I was living on the edge! I started experimenting with flavored creamers (always the large, door-sized versions): blueberry cobbler, vanilla creme, hazelnut, and pumpkin spice (only available near Thanksgiving).

So in this don't-step-on-the-carpet apartment with the chicken-jerky, alphabetically arranged spices, and nonfat everything, I had my quiet moments with my foofy coffee. These moments were all mine. These were my grown-up moments when I could have things exactly how I wanted them—me, the grown-up Sylvia.

Going home for weekends and holidays introduced me to new coffee. My parents did not keep gourmet coffee beans in the freezer; they had freeze-dried Taster's Choice on the counter. Over time, they developed a taste for a certain coffee shop, and a new routine was created. Dad would go out and buy two extra-large coffees in paper cups and bring them back. They were a special treat, and we used the coffee cups like carafes, pouring from them throughout the morning. Mom and Dad like their coffee black; there were no foofy creamers to choose from.

As I watched my parents make changes in their coffee consumption, it became clear that the process mirrored the way they arranged their lives together. Each time one or the other wanted to try a new coffee, the other one went along—sometimes reluctantly, sometimes enthusiastically—and in the end, they found a way to agree. I thought the large-cup-carafe thing was eccentric and impractical. The coffee didn't stay hot long enough, and I always imagined the inside liner of the paper cup seeping slowly into the beverage. But it worked for them, and that presented a beautiful, physical example of experimentation, compromise, and longevity in their relationship. While I stayed in their home, I should respect (if not embrace) the choices they made for themselves as a steadfast couple. My choices (my coffee) belonged outside the home into which I was born.

I didn't last long with April (the chicken-jerky girl), and chose the next apartment for the quirky, fun-loving roommates and the complete lack of carpeting. We had wood floors, paneled walls, and wood furniture. How I loved the wood! I kept my shoes on all day. I never ate broiled chicken. I made pots and pots of coffee and tried every creamer I could find. Eventually I married a man who loves coffee and wood floors (and dislikes dry broiled chicken) even more than I do. He drinks his coffee black, and I'm still indulging in sweet creamers. That's a joy of growing up: no one can tell you how to have your coffee.

Charlotte and Tita

"Your mother will never see you again if you do not marry Mr. Collins, and I will never see you again if you do." (Mr. Bennet)

-*Pride and Prejudice*, Jane Austen

We romantics have a lot to learn, of course, from Jane Austen. Love and marriage can be complicated, and do not always coincide. In *Pride and Prejudice*, Elizabeth Bennet must hold her tongue when her friend Charlotte Lucas settles down with the pitiful Mr. Collins, whom she herself has refused. He may be supercilious and unappealing, but he offers Charlotte a comfortable home and financial security. Charlotte is rapidly approaching spinsterhood, and Mr. Collins may be her last chance. Elizabeth must reconcile herself to the match, and learn not to impose her own values and opinions on her closest friend. The choice is not hers to make.

In *Like Water for Chocolate*, Laura Esquivel wrote of a love that would shock the petticoats off Ms. Austen: red-hot passion. Tita de la Garza is madly in love with Pedro Muzquiz, but forbidden to marry him. After Pedro marries another and moves away, Tita's life becomes unbearable. Tragedy strikes the family, and her cruel and tyrannical mother pushes Tita into a mental breakdown. Dr. Brown answers her mother's request to take Tita to an asylum, but instead whisks her away to his home and nurses her back to health with compassion, wisdom, and devotion. He has watched her grow up, seen her at her strongest and weakest, and saved her. When he proposes, she accepts. With him, she feels happy and at peace. Then Pedro returns, and Tita cannot resist the searing, magnetic heat that draws her back to him.

I, more a product of Jane's world than Laura's, would have chosen Dr. Brown in an instant. Ever the prudish romantic, during each of two dozen readings, I prayed for Tita to make a different choice. No such luck.

I met my Charlotte Lucas at my very first real job. It was the 1980s, the nadir of American fashion trends. Charlotte wore flowered dresses, large-rimmed glasses, and a bit too much eye shadow. She looked like an owl that had gone Hawaiian. New Jersey style. Still, as the two "kids" at the office, we became fast friends and lunch buddies. We always found things to talk about: being out on our own, getting our first apartments, and searching for interesting guys to date.

She was seeing Dan the Kid, who seemed never to need to shave, and who only felt romantic on Fridays. We dubbed my crush Pipsqueak Runt, because I stood a full head taller than him, and his voice sounded like he'd just inhaled helium. We joked about voice-casting them in a cartoon Western. A guinea pig wearing a ten-teaspoon hat, a holster, and a sheriff's badge stood at one end of a deserted street. Tumbleweeds rolled by.

They were twice his size. The hot sun blazed down, and he wiped his forehead with one furry paw. From a nearby saloon, Dan the Kid emerged wearing western boots with spurs, a chocolate milk mustache, and Superman Underoos. They stared each other down. "I dare you to draw," squeaked the sheriff.

"What? Speak up. I can't understand you!"

The guinea pig cleared his throat and tried to lower his voice. "I dare you to take out your weapon!"

"Oh! I can't do that," replied the Kid. "I only shoot on Fridays."

The year flew by, and we both moved away and on with our lives. Her career started to take off, I met and married David, and she rode the dating roller coaster without me. After Dan the Kid, she spent an entire year with Medical Man, who broke her heart. A short rebound relationship with The Football Fan helped her heal, and then she met Tyler. He received no sobriquet. She had found the gentlest, most well-meaning person she had ever met, and she loved him very much. One weekend I made the trek to Boston, where they were living, to catch up and meet her wonderful new man. We met for dinner at a Mexican restaurant and tried to get to know one another over Supreme Nachos. Ty was certainly adorable, but did not appear much more mature than Dan the Kid. He didn't have Charlotte's intellect, her work ethic, or her burgeoning sophistication. I just didn't get it.

The next day, Charlotte and I were browsing through a book fair when she gave me the big news: Tyler had proposed. She had not answered yet, but she loved him very much. She wanted to know what I thought of him. What could I say? How can, or should, a good friend answer that question? What

would Jane Austen have me say? Just because I was not impressed with him did not mean he couldn't make her happy.
I could tell my husband was not exactly her cup of tea, but
frankly it was none of her business. I knew he was right for me,
and her opinion could never convince me otherwise.

I balked. "He seems very sweet," I stammered. I picked up
a book and flipped the pages, trying to look intensely interested in, oh my, Indian cooking? Masala sauce requires twelve
ingredients. One of them is kosher salt. Why kosher salt? Since
when do Indians know about kosher salt? "Hey, Charlotte!
What makes salt *kosher*? Does a rabbi bless it? Do they kill the
salt in a humane way?"

Charlotte was not ready to change the subject. "What do
you think? Tell me!" she demanded.

"I think my palate isn't refined enough to tell the difference
between salts, anyway. Some people only cook with sea salt."

"I mean, what about Tyler?" she pressed.

"You're asking me? I don't know what kind of salt he uses!
Come on, I just met the guy."

"Sylvie, you know what I mean. What do you think of Tyler? What do you really think?"

I exhaled sharply. "Well, the restaurant was very noisy. He
sure likes nachos." Charlotte glared at me. "Okay, fine. He's
very sweet and polite. It's obvious he worships you. He's got
great taste! So, what's not to like?"

Lowering her voice and taking a step closer, she cut straight
to the chase: "Is David your great love and your great passion?"
We had discussed *Like Water for Chocolate* before.

"Yes," I replied without hesitation. Years before I met David, I'd fallen in love for the first time and thought that he was my great passion, like Pedro was for Tita. Our relationship was steamy and sincere, but it was also doomed by diverging values, interests, and expectations. When I met David, who represents to me the very essence of Dr. John Brown, the physicality of my first passion seemed insignificant.

Four months into my relationship with David, I had an operation. David stayed by my side every step of the way: emergency room, tests, surgery. He later admitted that seeing me in need made him realize that he loved me, that he wanted to take care of me, always. Of course I didn't know that then; I only knew the feeling of his hand in mine when I most needed a hand to hold.

The anesthesia left me groggy, intravenous fluids bloated me like a water balloon, and the stitches hurt a great deal. A smiling old lady watched the slow progress of my first postsurgery walk around the floor. I gingerly cradled my unusually large stomach in one hand, and gripped David's arm with the other. "It's so nice to see a young couple in love!" the woman called out. "Do you know yet if it's a girl or a boy?" David and I couldn't help but laugh awkwardly. "Actually," I replied, "it's an appendix!"

"What if Ty is my great love, but not my great passion?" Charlotte asked intensely. "Should I marry him? I couldn't bear to lose him."

"I can't answer that for you, Charlotte. You have to follow your heart. But I will tell you that if I had only one choice, between love and passion, I would choose love any day." I spoke what I felt, but after all, I had just turned twenty-five; I wasn't a wise hermit on a mountaintop. The question made me uneasy.

Charlotte did marry Ty, and I was a bridesmaid at their wedding. She looked elegant in her high-necked, long-sleeved, beaded gown (Jane Austen would have approved), though perhaps not as exuberant as a modern bride should be. She reminded me vaguely of my friend Miriam, who was also a little pale and stiff at her wedding. Miriam married at age twenty-six and was still a virgin. She had finally found herself the perfect man, and he, too, had waited until marriage. As her wedding day approached, Miriam busied herself with details of seating arrangements and music selections, but I could tell something else was bothering her: she was deathly afraid of her wedding night. She denied it, but she was. In fact, she had worked herself up into such a frenzy, she came down with an illness the day before the wedding.

Of course the wedding couldn't be postponed; her parents had gone all-out for their darling daughter's nuptials. Three hundred guests were expected at their fancy, hotel shindig. One banquet hall opened an hour before the ceremony for hors d'oeuvres and champagne; the flowers and ice sculptures alone could have bought her a car. Another hall had been set up with dinner tables and a large dance floor, and of course a third room had been decked out with flowers, and chairs covered in white slipcovers, for the actual ceremony. This party had cost a fortune and was expected to last all night. As they say on Broadway, "The show must go on!"

When I saw Miriam just half an hour before she said "I do," her gown was covered with towels and her mother was applying yet another coat of makeup to her pasty, sweaty face. "She's got a 102-degree fever," one of the bridesmaids whispered in my ear. "She was puking all morning, but you can't postpone a wedding like this!" She opened the door a crack and peeked at the crowds milling about with champagne glasses. "There must be two hundred people here already!" Just then, someone yanked the door open and thrust a white paper bag at the bridesmaid. "Here, biggest bottle of Pepto they've got! Let her chug it!"

The makeup and Pepto seemed to do the trick. Miriam looked lovely walking down the aisle and in the photos, though she did not dance during the reception. The extravagant party went on for hours with a six-piece band with a singer, incredible food, open bar, and a fading bride. I felt sorry for Miriam, who had dreamt all her life about her perfect wedding. Now she had it, every bit as glamorous as she could have hoped for, but she could not enjoy it. Her new husband cancelled their Hawaii honeymoon and drove Miriam to her mother's house to recuperate for a week. When she recovered, she finally moved in with her husband and learned she had made herself sick with fear for nothing: he was impotent.

Charlotte did not get sick at her wedding. She looked pale, and perhaps a little nervous, but Ty grinned at her like a love-sick puppy until she laughed and threw her arms around him. She danced with everyone at the reception, and left straight away for their honeymoon. I went back to my happily-ever-after, and other than a postcard from the Bahamas, did not hear from Charlotte at all. Months passed, and then one day I got The Phone Call:

"I need to ask Ty for a divorce."

Oh my! This came out of nowhere. I couldn't imagine why she'd need a divorce. I assumed she'd gone radio-silent like most new brides do, because they were enjoying their new routine, setting up a new apartment, and lazing around on weekends. "What happened?"

Charlotte took a long, deep breath. "I don't love him the way I need to love him. I adore him, he's my best friend, but I can't stand it when he touches me." She began to cry, desperately hoping to hear some miraculous solution to her problem. "I thought maybe the passion would come after a while. We'd never slept together; I thought it would be OK after we were married. You know, like Tita would have been with Dr. Brown, if Pedro hadn't shown up."

Charlotte had been just as nervous as Miriam! Even though she'd had experience with other men, her relationship with Ty had been innocent. Charlotte told me Ty wasn't her great passion, but I had never imagined there might be no passion at all! I wondered how women managed in Jane Austen's day, those innocent daughters of gentlemen, who perhaps had no idea what they were getting into. I hope the men were patient and gentle with them. I'm sure Ty had been patient and gentle; he clearly adored her. This situation was horribly tragic, and the only way for Charlotte to have a happy future would be to break a solemn vow and destroy the hopes of her dearest friend, who had believed she loved him, and who had counted on 'forever.'

Charlotte knew she couldn't stay with Ty; that would slowly kill her. She wanted to avoid hurting him but couldn't see how. "If I tell him I'm not attracted to him, that I never was, it will destroy him. He's so insecure. How can I do that to my best friend? He thinks I'm having an affair, and that's why I don't want him to touch me. I'm going to let him think that. Then he can hate me and not himself. After all, this is my fault, not his."

Soon after, they divorced. As time passed and Charlotte began to process what had happened, she guessed at my secret: I had not thought Ty was right for her. Grudgingly, I admitted it. She became angry that I had hidden my feelings from her. She depended on my judgment, always trusted my intuition. If I had been a true friend, I would have spoken up, and could have spared her all of this pain. She would have found a way to refuse the proposal and still remain friends. Months of misery, Ty's humiliation at being so quickly divorced…I could have prevented all of it! My fault!

Why hadn't I told her what I really felt about Ty? After all, she had asked for an honest opinion. I did have an opinion: she needed more than he could provide. She was an accomplished young woman, but he was still a boy. Perhaps I could have prevented her pain, if I'd had been more courageous and less… polite. I had always heard that caution should triumph over opinion when it comes to giving friends love advice. If you speak ill of a boyfriend who then becomes the husband, your friendship is over. Better to hope you're wrong and stay close by to pick up the pieces in case you're not. Years after Charlotte's divorce, David and I once hit a short, bumpy patch. Charlotte let her hair down and made some unflattering remarks about him. While I often joke that I'm blessed with a memory as reliable as a sieve for a bucket, I will never forget those biting words about the man with whom I have happily spent more than twenty years of my life.

Austen's Charlotte Lucas may have had to marry Mr. Collins, but my twentieth century Charlotte would have many opportunities to find a better suitor. Charlotte found a man who is both her great passion and her great love, and I'm glad she didn't have to choose just one of the two. In honor of that marriage, I stopped rereading *Like Water for Chocolate* and pining for Dr. Brown. Tita wouldn't appreciate my coming between her and Pedro. She would adore him regardless of common sense, gratitude, or admiration. And as for my Charlotte, perhaps I should have helped her kick Mr. Collins out the door. I'll never know for sure, but deep in my heart I believe the choice wasn't mine to make.

A Friend in Need
(Becomes a Friend Indeed)

No way around it, no way to avoid it: fate had dumped me into a freshman dorm for my senior year in college. Jaded and oh-so "over it," I dragged my suitcase past the gaggle of yapping, perky chihuahuas by the water fountain and headed to the left. At least my room—one of the two doubles reserved for hapless upperclassmen—was right by the hall phone and close to the door to the stairs. I planned to sneak in and out without ever introducing myself.

My roommate had not arrived yet. I heaved my suitcase onto the bed furthest from the door and wondered whether to unpack. Maybe the housing office would call tomorrow and tell me they'd made a mistake; I could move into a senior apartment like I'd planned, after all!

Maybe I shouldn't blame fate, either. After all, Jessica had done this to me. She had been my closest friend at school for two years! We had studied together, talked about boys together. I counted on her to submit my paperwork for housing while I was away for junior year, but she couldn't be bothered that day.

The deadline passed, and my name went down to the bottom of the list. Some friend she'd turned out to be. I began to hope my roommate—Allison, according to the sign on the door—would be less of a disaster for me.

The suspense had just started to build when Allison arrived. Hurray! She was a senior, too! We commiserated over being stuck with the chihuahuas and compared notes on how it had happened. She had planned to share an apartment off-campus with a friend, but the girl bailed out on her at the last minute. Pretty similar to my story, and just as painful. Allison and I had both been burned by what she called "junk food friends." Junk foods look appealing in the package and taste great going down, but you can't count on them to sustain you. We'd learned that lesson the hard way.

Our unfortunate choice of housing advocates was the only thing Allison and I had in common, but we got along well. Since the phone hung right next to our door, we became the hall note-takers. It was always for one of chihuahuas, who were easy prey for upperclass frat brothers. We'd run down the hall, rap on whoever's door, run back down the hall, and ask to take a message, which we then had to write on whoever's dry-erase board with the hearts-and-stars border in pink and purple. After a while, we got tired of taking their messages. "Just let it ring," Allison eventually suggested. "Someone else will get it if we don't."

So the next morning, I let it ring. It rang twelve times before the caller gave up. A few minutes later, it started ringing again. Someone really wanted to reach a chihuahua; what should I do? I took pity on the caller and picked up the phone. This time it wasn't a frat boy; it sounded like someone's mother. "Is Kelli there? That's Kelli with an "i" in room 208." I walked down the hall and knocked, then returned to the caller. "Sorry, she's out. Can I take a message?" No, she didn't want to leave a message; she'd rather pelt me with a million questions!

Twenty-eight minutes later, I managed to get off the phone politely. That's longer than I talked to my own mother, and I didn't even know this woman. I didn't want to know this woman, or her freshman daughter, Kelli with an "i". I stomped down to Kelli's door and wrote a note without signing it: "Your mom called."

That night Kelli came knocking on the door. "Hey, thanks for taking that message," she smiled. "My mom told me what a great talk you and she had. She hopes we're going to be great friends." I smiled back, made some excuse about meeting people in the library, and escaped down the stairs. I couldn't risk getting stuck in another twenty-eight minute conversation when I had a paper to write!

When I returned around ten o'clock, Allison was heading out for a party. This would be the pattern for the entire semester: I went to bed, she went out. She came home, I ran off to breakfast.

Most of the chihuahuas were out late every night, too—but not Kelli with an "i." The second time Kelli knocked on my door, she needed a phone number. "Do you know a pizza place that delivers? I'm famished!" We shared a pineapple pizza in her room, since she kept her minifridge stocked with Fresca. It never occurred to me that we might actually have some things in common (e.g. love of Fresca), or that any girl at school could be dorkier than me.

Kelli liked chemistry (eww). She had everything laid out on her desk at right angles. She strung multicolored Christmas lights on her wall around an oversized poster of a pink Cadillac. In short, she had me beat on the dork-o-meter.

Kelli reminded me of spinach. The first time you eat spinach, you're not sure you ever want to try it again, but your mom makes you. Over time, you quit grimacing and start to enjoy it, in part because you know deep down that it's good for you. I hadn't wanted to meet Kelli, but her mom "made me," and now I found out that she was actually good for me. To Kelli, I was not a dull, no-fun girl. She actually laughed at my jokes! She didn't find my rambling insights and analogies confusing. With Kelli, I could be a new person—not because I had changed, but because she saw me differently than other people did.

One night I heard a frantic knocking at my door. There stood Kelli, with a campus security officer behind her. "Can you come with me?" she asked, tears in her eyes. "I really need you." As the officer escorted us across the dark campus, I tried to ask for an explanation, but she just shook her head and kept walking. The officer finally led us into a small building. We squinted at the harsh light as our eyes adjusted from being outside, and the fluorescent bulbs buzzed and flickered eerily above our heads. I'd never been in this building before, and couldn't imagine how someone as squeaky clean as Kelli could be in so much trouble.

As we sat on a faded flame-stitch couch, I noticed a plaque bearing the words "Psychology Department." At least now I knew where we were. Kelli leaned over and whispered in my ear, "OK, here's the deal: see, Mom and I got in an argument, and she sort of wigged out and told the school I might commit suicide. The security guard tracked me down and pulled me out of the movie theatre in front of everyone! It was so humiliating, you have no idea…"

At that moment, the door opened and a skinny, balding man in a rumpled shirt greeted us. "Hey, there." Then, noticing Kelli's bloodshot eyes, he said, "You must be Kelli. And this is…?"

"She's my friend. She's here to be with me."

"OK, that's fine. Come in and make yourselves comfortable." We entered his office and lowered ourselves into upholstered wing chairs. The psychiatrist crossed one leg over the other. His jeans were inches too short, and he was wearing white tube socks with brown loafers. What a dork.

"Well, Kelli, I think you know why you're here. Your mother was concerned that you might hurt yourself. I'm here to make sure you're safe."

Kelli shifted in her seat. "Thanks, but I'm not the sick one. Mom's the one who has problems, not me. That's why I brought my friend, Sylvia, for a character witness." She paused to look at me, and I nodded reassuringly. "You see, my mother is an alcoholic. And she's…not well. She relies on me so much, and she didn't want me to go away to school. One way or another, she's determined to get me back home so I can take care of her. But I want a life of my own. Please, I'm fine. I don't need to go to a hospital, and I really don't want to go home."

An hour later, Dr. Tube Socks let us walk out, without the security guard. "Thanks for coming tonight," Kelli said. "I really needed a friend. You're a good friend."

Our relationship changed that night. Rather than dragging myself down the hall in lonely desperation to knock on her door, I actually began to seek out Kelli's company. What I had considered a small favor had won me loyalty for life.

I'd helped Kelli, and she found a way to help me in return. When she heard my story about Jessica and the housing fiasco, she became outraged. "You're the greatest friend ever! She doesn't deserve your friendship. Did you even tell her how you feel?" I admitted that I had not seen her all semester and saw no reason to confront her: what was done could not be undone.

"That much is true," she agreed, "but don't just be a victim! You have to stand up for yourself. You have to, because you can." I understood what she meant. She wished she could stand up to her mother, but her situation was far more complicated than mine. In a weird way, my standing up to Jess would make us both feel better.

We talked about what I should say and imagined what Jess would say in return. Eventually I felt prepared to face her without backing down. I didn't do the best job in the world, but Kelli and I celebrated the attempt with pineapple pizza and Fresca.

Sometimes we choose our friends, and sometimes they are thrust upon us. For two years running, I had not only chosen Jessica as a friend but publicized to all who would hear it that she was my "best friend." Then she failed me the one time I really needed her. Because of her, I spent my senior year in a freshman dorm, and that makes her junk food. As for Kelli, I may have felt stuck with her at first, but she turned out to be spinach. She made me strong.

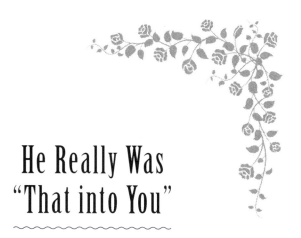

He Really Was
"That into You"

*Algernon: You'll never break off our engagement
again, Cecily?*
*Cecily: I don't think I could break it off now that
I have actually met you.*

- *The Importance of Being Earnest*, Oscar Wilde

In the 2009 film *He's Just Not That into You*, Ben Affleck does not want to marry his long-time girlfriend played by Jennifer Anniston. He behaves like a husband—better, in fact, than her sisters' husbands—and loves her unconditionally. But "marriage" does not interest him. *Spoiler alert!* Jennifer's character finally tells him she will accept the relationship as it is. That should be enough, movie-goers! Happy ending. But no: Ben ends up down on one knee. Now, I'm a die-hard romantic, but this goes too far. In a time of fifty-percent marriage failure, do we really care if she gets a ring? Isn't it more important that we believe they have a chance at happiness?

I was devastated when Tim Robbins and Susan Sarandon called it quits, and they were never even married. That made the whole situation even more poignant. Two cooler people never existed, and they had stayed together because they wanted to be together. The more I thought about it, the more I could accept the new reality. They had spent a huge part of their lives together. Nothing had failed; they were just ready to move on. If they both felt that way, I should be happy for them, happy they had enjoyed so many good years, and hopeful that they find happiness again, with or without partners.

My friend—let's call her "Bennie"—could have been a character in that "Bennifer" movie. She really wanted a white wedding. I met Bennie in law school, though she didn't seem to belong there any more than I did. Only five years my senior, she dressed much older, and wore her bangs too short and cut straight across her forehead. She read classic books, listened to Beethoven, and had studied music in her native Jackson, Mississippi. Bennie's parents split up when she was young, and money had always been tight. Because of a bad back, her mother slept not on a bed but in a lounge chair in the living room. It sounded so sad: raising a child all by herself, deep in the conservative South, sleeping in a chair. Never quite comfortable enough, I imagined, in any way. Bennie was determined to excel and never to rely on anyone for what she needed.

Bennie and I found each other during orientation. We got season tickets to the ballet together, went out for coffee, and talked between classes. Once again I'd managed to find someone so wonderfully bland, I seemed exotic and interesting in comparison. She befriended some polite, dedicated international students, while I gathered a motley crew of American misfits around me. Then one day, my most unconventional friend asked me a surprising question: "Hey! Who is that girl you hang around with, the one with the great legs?"

I looked around the room. "Who? Maria?"

"No!" he said. "That one over there, in the maroon cardigan and the granny skirt."

He motioned towards Bennie. I tried not to look shocked. Don't tell me Julian—sexy, moody, rock-and-roll Julian—could be interested in her! That match would last a day at most. He stayed up all night and slept half the day. He liked loud, gritty, angry music and hated just about everything else. Julian came to law school because his wealthy, philandering father had agreed to pay for it, and because his brilliant mind needed something to keep itself occupied. He had a mass of black curly hair, and bedroom eyes that barely peeked out from under his thick, long eyelashes. He reeked of sensuality, intensity, and danger. "You have got to be kidding me," I replied. "Well, that's Bennie."

Next thing I knew, he had asked her out. To a concert. Not to the orchestra, mind you, but to some grunge band performing at midnight in a remote bar I'd be afraid to enter in broad daylight. She actually liked it! Granny skirts disappeared and were replaced by faded jeans and T-shirts. She giggled like a teenager with puppy love. In return, Julian would open doors for her, whisper compliments in her ear, and show up for classes before noon. (Well, sometimes.)

As I watched them bumble through the early stages of romance, I remained convinced that each date would be their last. For Valentine's Day, he presented her with a cactus, because roses are too unoriginal. A cactus! I remember the time my father gave my mother an electric screwdriver for Valentine's

Day. I had shrunk in fear, waiting for the angry screams, but to my surprise, my mother loved the screwdriver. And sure enough, Bennie adored her cactus. I began to think anything was possible.

Almost three years later, graduation day loomed before them like a guillotine. She had accepted a position at a top law firm in Washington, DC; he had taken a government job in a small New England town. "Come with me," he had asked her. "It will be easier for you to find a job there, than for me to fit in with the DC crowd. Your grades are better, you present yourself better. You're amazing. Just come with me, and we'll be happy forever. I promise. We won't need much. Just a nice little house and each other."

Oh. My. Stars.

By this point I had already become engaged to David (and dropped out of law school), but even I could drool over this Hollywood ending. Gorgeous, dreamy drifter falls head over heels for a woman who gives him stability for the first time in his life. Conservative woman lets her hair down and finds passion and true love. They live out their days in total bliss, reading Shakespeare, listening to hard rock, and making love until the sun rises. The camera pans the room. Mozart concerto on the piano bench, which is draped in a black concert T-shirt. Beer can on the table, with a coaster. Cactus on the windowsill, wrapped in a red silk ribbon. Fade to black. "...And they lived happily ever after."

"Oh my Gd!" I shrieked into the phone. "And what did you say?"

"Well, I asked him to marry me." Uh-oh.

I knew Julian had problems with the idea of marriage. His parents' marriage had been a disaster and ended in an ugly divorce. A tux and white gown circus did not mesh with his antiestablishment bravado. But I did believe that he loved Bennie completely, and that he would be true to her. He would never repeat his father's mistakes, never become that which he despised. Did he agree to marry her? "Well?" I asked anxiously.

"He...I....I'm giving him until graduation to think about it. If I get a ring, I will turn down my job offer and follow him to the ends of the earth. But I'm not going without one. I'm not going to end up like my mother, all alone."

"But Bennie! You won't be alone. He's not going to leave you. Your mom had a ring. A ring will not make him stay with you. If anything, it'll push him away! This is your chance at love. At first I couldn't picture you together, but I was wrong. You are meant to be together. Go! Go follow him, and be happy."

"I'll see if I get a ring. He has until graduation. I'd be giving up a lot for him. He needs to do this for me. If he really loves me, he'll do it."

Love cannot be defined. Love should not be given ultimatums. Needless to say, Bennie did not get her ring, but not because he didn't love her. The weekend I married David—the weekend Bennie should have been my bridesmaid—she busied herself unpacking boxes into her new DC apartment, alone, while Julian moved north without her. How ironic! While I felt my life just beginning, her world had come crashing down on her. I hadn't known, of course, when I asked her to be in our wedding. I asked her way before the ultimatum. Before she gave up on love, perhaps forever.

There's a saying, "If you love someone, set them free." How about this instead: if you love someone, love all of him, not just the parts that are like you. Bennie had fallen in love with a rebel, and threw him away because he could not change for her. Certainly there were enough conservative preachers' sons in Jackson, Mississippi who would marry a great girl like Bennie, but they hadn't appealed to her. She loved Julian in part because he was so different from everything she had ever known, and then she left him for the same reason. Bennie believed she was being strong and protecting herself. I believe she acted out of fear, and that is not strength.

Four years later, our paths crossed briefly. David and I had moved back to Atlanta. Bennie came into town on business, and we met for lunch before she headed to the airport. The last time I'd seen her, she was all Julian, pizza, and beer. Now she had returned to egg salad and unsweetened tea. She told us about her job, the long hours, the furniture she planned to buy for her apartment when she had the time. She had her career but nothing else: no friends, no hobbies, no boyfriend, no exotic vacations, no time. No joy.

I would like to believe that in some alternate universe, Bennie took the gamble, and that she and Julian bought a tiny little love nest and spent snowy winters snuggling by an old brick fireplace. That she found a job that allowed her enough free time for playing the piano, going to the theater, and traveling with Julian to exotic locations. That Julian met and loved her mother, and that she loved him in return.

We all have our fears and our crosses to bear. It would be unfair of me to judge Bennie. I would have been devastated if David didn't want to marry me, but David was not a rebel. David's refusal would have meant I wasn't "the one," while Julian's was simply an extension of who he was, part of why she fell in love with him. I believed in him and that they would be happy together. Though I wish she had chosen differently, it was not my gamble to make.

Sometimes when we try to avoid our fate, we end up creating it. Fearing a future of being alone, Bennie gave up true love. Whether she will ever marry, I do not know. I hope that if she does, she marries for love and not just for company. Love takes courage, Bennie! Love takes risks. I hope you can be brave.

Giving from the Heart

When I was younger, some people described me as a walking heart. I cried at Hallmark commercials. I cried at the end of *Miracle on 34th Street*. I cried when I was happy, and when I was sad. I cried at bar mitzvahs, graduations, weddings, and funerals. I think it would have been more accurate to say I was a walking faucet, because I've met many other people with more obvious heart.

Our former dog groomer, Mary, is one such person. Just barely getting by herself, she always found ways to give to others. She cared for the sick and the elderly. She helped friends paint their houses or weed their gardens. She adopted stray dogs. She helped friends pack up and move. She painted, cleaned, hauled, nursed, fed, and took care of people whether or not her electricity had been turned off, whether or not she was back on food stamps. I've never met anyone with a bigger heart.

I could always relate to Mary. We are both constantly grateful for the little things in life. We both love our dogs, worship our children, and look for the rainbow in every gray sky. Like me, she cries freely and without shame. Is she a Pisces, too? I'll have to ask her.

Anyway, Mary loves to talk, especially about her daughters. Every six weeks or so, I'd get another earful. Tina was only twelve, and Crystal had just turned eighteen. Although Crystal was extremely bright, she suffered from a combination of unmedicated ADD and a typical teen-age attitude of (unwarranted) superiority. She graduated from high school early and took a job as a nurse's aide.

Unsatisfied and restless, Crystal began to consider opportunities in the navy. (Her late father had served in the navy.) She placed very high on the assessment examination and received an offer from the Intelligence Department. There would be a lot of training, and of course she'd have to leave home, but when she finished the program she'd command a higher salary than she'd ever dreamed possible. Their financial worries would soon be over. Or would they?

Six months before her basic training, Crystal found out she was pregnant. So much for starting in the spring! She had to put the navy on hold, at least for a year or two, or maybe forever. For the meantime she moved in with the baby's father, who lived in a neighboring county. He was an apprentice house painter and lived in an ancient trailer behind his mother's home. His mother was accustomed to free access to both her son and the trailer, and constantly barged in unannounced. Crystal had no privacy, personal space, or time to consider her options.

As Crystal's belly grew, so did her discontent. "Can't say I blame her," Mary told me. "I wish Kyle had a house of his own. I saw the trailer, and it's a dump. They're saving up for a place of their own, but they're short two thousand for the down payment. I hate the thought of my grandbaby living in that horrid trailer, with that horrible woman barging in at all hours, cigarette dangling from her mouth. This is not a grandmother's dream, I assure you."

Mary looked positively miserable. "What if it was possible to get a long-term, no-interest loan?" I asked innocently.

"They don't have enough credit for any loan, and there's no such thing as no-interest!"

"Just let me talk to David. He knows a lot of people. Let me see what I can do, OK? No promises. I'll swing by the shop in a couple of days and let you know if we can help."

Mary's eyes filled with tears. "Thank you so much for caring. If there's anything you can do, that would be great. I want my baby out of there. And my grandbaby, when it comes!"

That night I told David about Mary's problem. "Couldn't we loan them the money? It would be such a big help to them. Crystal and Kyle could get a nice place, and Mary could stop worrying about them."

"Didn't you tell me Crystal was going to join the navy?" David asked.

"Well, yes, but that was before the baby came into the picture."

"Are they holding her spot? Can't she go to basic training in a couple of years? Can one of the grandmothers look after the baby? I'm sure Mary would love to do it."

"I don't know if Crystal has given up on the navy idea. Besides, she needs a place now," I insisted.

"I think the navy is the best thing that could happen to that family," David countered. "Let's face it: they're always just barely scraping by. You have no idea who this Kyle guy is, or whether he'll marry her, or whether they will stay together. They're just kids! If Crystal is locked into some home or condo, she's much less likely to join the navy. And what about the monthly payments? Believe me, you wouldn't be doing her any favors by loaning her the money."

With a heavy heart, I stopped by the grooming shop and told Mary we couldn't help. She took it well, but I felt terrible about it. I couldn't imagine my daughter living in a beat-up trailer in someone's backyard. I wouldn't want my grandbaby raised there. Poor Mary. Poor Crystal.

David and I often helped people when money became an obstacle, so why couldn't we now? When a friend needed backing for his new business, we didn't hesitate to make the loan. When our nanny's sister called at three in the morning needing bail money for her husband, David immediately dressed and ran out to the ATM. I once overheard my daughter's preschool teacher say her husband was working extra shifts to pay for their children's Catholic school tuition. David didn't blink when I made an anonymous donation to their account at that school, and he'd never even met them! Why wouldn't he let me help Mary's daughter? Men just don't understand.

As I said, I felt miserable. Then, before any ring was purchased and before the baby was born, Crystal and Kyle separated! Crystal moved back home to have her baby, and Mary is the happiest, proudest grandmother I have ever met. "Thank goodness they didn't buy a property together," she told me. "It would have complicated everything." Last I heard, Crystal was contacting the navy to set a schedule for her training.

David could have said "I told you so," but I'm glad he didn't. He already knew what I had to learn: while giving in simple ways (like a shoulder to cry on or a ride to the auto shop) can be done at a moment's notice, life-altering assistance (like financing a home purchase) should never be done without a great deal of consideration.

My heart is always in the right place. It's just that sometimes brain has to come before heart. I will never again complain when David tries to rationally analyze what I believe to be a "heart" decision. Heart alone can be a dangerous thing, and should be left to experts like Mary. Mary, who has mastered the art of making a huge difference one tiny step at a time. Mary, who improves the lives of everyone she meets, and accepts their love in return. That's why even when she's broke, she's the richest woman in the world.

Bad Sir Brian Botany

*"The good ended happily, and the bad unhappily.
That is what Fiction means."*

-*The Importance of Being Earnest*, Oscar Wilde

"Sir Brian had a battleaxe with great big knobs on.

*He went among the villagers and blipped
them on the head."*

- A.A. Milne

Poor villagers! Poor Sir Brian. He didn't really know what he was doing, or he wouldn't have behaved that way. He certainly wouldn't have "blipped" the villagers had he been able to see the future, for the villagers take away his battleaxe and get their revenge! Sir Brian learns his lesson and reinvents himself, but he is a character in a children's poem, not a real person. Real-life bullies don't always get "blipped" back. Real-life bullies don't always reform. My friend Amy met a bully once, but her Sir Brian had no battleaxe. In fact, he was armed only with a pocket-protector and an attitude.

Brian arrived at the Y wearing polyester pants and a short-sleeved, button-down shirt, tucked in without a belt. He emerged from the locker room without improving his image. Now he sported a faded gray t-shirt with a hole in it, bright blue shorts, and white socks pulled high from his black tennies to his knobby knees. Brian had a diploma from a two-year computer tech college, and one crooked tooth on top, two teeth right of center. Brian also exuded extraordinary confidence, likely springing from the fact that he was the only one over age thirty in a singles volleyball league filled with very recent college grads.

It was soon obvious to everyone except Amy that Brian had his eye on her. He would watch her play, offer encouragement and make sure she was first at the water cooler after the match. He was an awkward, horrible volleyball player, and an awkward, horrible suitor. Amy politely ignored him when we all went out to the diner, even though he always grabbed the seat next to her every time.

Week after week he pursued her until she at last noticed. One afternoon on the way out of the diner, he asked her out. "No thanks," she replied. "I'm really busy right now. This league is all I have time for."

"I'm not talking about anything serious," said Brian. "Just dinner one night. You have to eat dinner, right? Let me take you to dinner."

"I'm really not wanting to date anyone right now, Brian. I see you every week."

"Come on, just as friends. Just dinner! I know this great Greek restaurant."

"No, thanks."

"How about Wednesday? They have live music on Wednesdays. Do you like Greek food?"

"Yes, I like Greek food. No, I'm not going out with you."

"I'm not letting you leave until you say you'll meet me for dinner."

"Brian, I said 'no thanks.' "

"So I'll meet you there at eight on Wednesday. How's that? Just friends."

"Yeah, fine. OK. I'll meet you there."

On Thursday Amy and I met after work so I could hear about their nondate. "How was it?" I needed to know. "Did Sir Brian turn out to be a frog or a prince?"

Well, the restaurant was really good, actually, and the music was fun. These men danced in a line and actually smashed plates on the floor, just like they do in the movies. At one point all the restaurant patrons were invited to join hands and dance along; she and Brian "opah-ed" with strangers and laughed until their sides split. Brian behaved like a gentleman, and if only she were maybe a million years older and not so allergic to polyester, it wouldn't have been that bad.

I laughed in reply. I still couldn't believe she'd been stuck with him for the whole evening, but in a way that was typical Amy. She'd rather deal with an evening of Sir Brian than make a scene telling him to take a hike. Truthfully, she was too sweet for her own good. Her parents used to fight all the time when she was growing up, and she had learned that keeping quiet and agreeing to everything kept her safe from their anger. She became the consummate "good girl." Her parents chose her clothes, her friends, her college, even her major. Eventually she took a job she was too good for, because her parents liked the company. We all know people like Amy, suffering with their halos.

"Well, at least that's over. You'll never have to see him again."

Silence.

"I said, you'll never have to see him again, right?"

"He sort of invited me over on Friday night. He wants to cook me dinner."

I didn't reply. If she was going to start dating Polyester Man. I wasn't going to say anything. None of my business.

"It's just dinner," she murmured. "Just as friends. It's not like I could say no or anything, after he'd been so nice."

Rrrrring! My phone rang on Saturday morning. Eight o'clock on Saturday morning. No one gets up at eight o'clock on Saturday morning, not even me! I let it ring. The answering machine clicked on, then clicked off again. *Rrrrring*! Okay, fine; someone really wanted to reach me. "Hullo?" I grunted into the phone. It was Amy. She wanted me to come over. Now. "Yeah, just let me throw on some sweats. I'll be right there." I stumbled around looking for keys and shoes, and managed to get over to Amy's without coffee or a shower.

Amy opened the door and threw her arms around me. She shook with sobs. I dropped my bag and keys on the floor and hugged her back. Eventually, the sobs died down. She loosened her grip on me, locked the door behind us, and took a seat on the sofa. Piles of tissues were scattered everywhere, and her eyes were red and swollen. "Oh my goodness, Amy. What happened?"

"I slept with Brian."

Oh. My. Oh. My. "Did he...did he—?"

"No!" She sobbed even louder. "He didn't make me. That makes it even worse! I didn't say no! I didn't say it at all! I mean, he wanted to, and he had been so nice and everything." She blew her nose loudly. "I'm such a loser! I didn't tell him not to. I feel like he...but he didn't, I mean, I didn't tell him not to! But I feel so dirty! So horrible! I'm so disgusting! I want to rip my skin right off and die!"

I stayed with Amy all day. We found another box of Kleenex and I made some tea. Tea always works in the movies. "Here, have some tea." I watched her cradle the warm mug in both hands. The steam drifted up onto her face, and she closed her eyes. One sip. Two sips. She sighed, allowing the warmth of the hot liquid to distract her momentarily from her misery. We sat silently, her sipping with her head down, me looking at the top of her head. Eventually I got really hungry, went to the kitchen, and made us some toast. She wouldn't eat a thing.

When night came, I ordered a pizza. Amy hadn't said a word for hours. I had been afraid to open my mouth, to say the wrong thing, or in any event, to start her off sobbing again. "Want some pizza?" She shook her head. I dug in, poured myself a Diet Coke, and decided it was time for me to say something profound, but I couldn't think of a thing.

"Y'know, Amy," I began, "just because you didn't say 'no' doesn't mean he didn't take advantage of you. He's a lot older. He knows how sweet you are, and probably figured he could get you to say 'yes.' You never really wanted to go out with him, and you told him that! He's a jerk. It's not your fault."

"Yeah, well, maybe so, but all it would have taken from me was one little word. One word and maybe he would have listened. Maybe not, but I'll never know, will I? 'Cause I never said it, and now it's over, and it's my fault because I didn't say it." She looked at me intently for a while, but I didn't know what she needed me to say.

"I'm so sorry, Amy. I'm sorry this happened."

"Yeah. Me, too."

Needless to say, Amy dropped out of the volleyball league. The very next week, I saw Brian there with another girl, whom I'd never seen before. Someone told me it was his old girlfriend. They had been really serious, maybe even engaged, and now they were getting back together. What a jerk, I thought to myself. A little conquest with a sweet, young girl, and now he's ready to get engaged to someone else? What's up with that? She wasn't even pretty, this other woman. She was old, too—at least thirty—and as nerdy as he was. I was fuming mad and had no one to tell. I couldn't mention it to Amy; it would have been too painful. Instead I, too, dropped out of the volleyball league and found other things to do with my spare time.

Amy moved away and we lost touch. I wonder about her sometimes, and whether she ever learned to speak her mind. What happened the next time she met a Brian? I know a woman who travels a lot for work. She wears her great-grandmother's wedding band whenever she leaves town so that she appears married. Even that doesn't always stop men from hitting on her, but then she can shake her head sadly, hold up her left hand, and point to the ring. Maybe Amy got a ring.

I wonder if this new generation still has Amys in it. Girls these days appear to have so much confidence. But do they really? Do they say no, or do they not say no, but for different reasons—like, to be popular? What do people teach their daughters these days? Amy's parents did not likely have "teach your daughter to be a pushover" as an objective, but somehow the message got through. She could have learned it at school, from being bullied. Heaven forbid, it could even be genetic. And while we're on the subject, I wonder what people teach their sons, now that chivalry is considered out-of-date. Does Brian even know he hurt Amy? Does he care?

My daughter Caitlin will never be an Amy. I'm not taking credit for it; she just is the way she is. Sometimes I worry she'll chase all the kids away; she gets so stubborn about things. "No, I don't wanna play that!" In time, she will learn about compromise, taking turns, and sharing. But she will always be a girl who knows what she wants, and how to be vocal and strong about it. She would never go out with a Brian, and no Brian would dare approach her. If a Brian laid a hand on her, she'd deck him with a two-knuckle punch. (She takes ballet *and* karate.)

Maybe being a grown-up means learning to balance "nice" with "I count, too." Maybe to be strong, you need to learn to put "I count" before "nice", so "I count" doesn't get lost along the way. Brian and Amy each learned just half the lesson, different halves. I hope it's not too late, for either of them.

Sharing Colors

I believe in angels, something good in everything I see

I believe in angels, when I know the time is right for me

I'll cross the stream...I have a dream.

Lyrics by ABBA (B. Andersson, B. Ulvaeus)

When we are little, the world appears almost blindingly bright in color and possibilities. All except good and evil, of course, which appear in black and white. "Oh, he lied once. He's bad!" "Oh, she shared her brownie. She's good!" When we grow older, we learn that there is also a lot of gray: even bad people sometimes share their brownies.

I have met many women who, after a divorce, see the world in black and white. All color —joy, excitement, hope— fades to nothing. The ex-husband is the bad guy, the guy in the black hat with the curly mustache and the gold tooth. The ex-wife is the angel dressed in white, having put up with more than most people could withstand, finally giving up on reforming the Black Hat in order to make a better life for herself (and her kids, if there are any). Sometimes these women are right, but sometimes their pain has masked the gray areas that would make them uncomfortable. Until they reconcile their emotions, the clouds never break, the sun never shines through, and their lives remain colorless.

Finding color again would be almost impossible without friends, like when we're little kids sharing Crayola's to make a picture. One friend might have the Cornflower Blue you wanted for a butterfly, and another, just the right shade of green for early spring grass. The more friends share with you, the more options you have, and the prettier your picture becomes. If you are willing to try multiple colors at once, even the grass gains depth and texture. You don't need fancy oil paints or pastels; just plain old crayons will do. The trick is, of course, that no one will share with you unless you share your colors in return.

I once met a woman whose life had lost all its color. She was an artist, an observer of life with a huge heart that had been badly broken. Life had started out all fireworks for Faith. She had a happy childhood, a close family, loads of confidence, and talent. In college she met a fun-loving, handsome guy and married him. The newlyweds moved to the west coast and found jobs that allowed them lots of free time to look at the ocean. They played at being grown-ups, and their life together offered a kaleidoscope of people, opportunities, and good times.

One day her husband decided it was time to settle down "for real" and join his father's construction company. They moved to his small, southern hometown and started a family of their own. Jeff's father owned the hotel, the restaurant, the convenience store, and much of the other property in town, and he built Faith and Jeff a large home abutting his own at the golf course. They enjoyed dinners at the country club, luxurious vacations, frequent spending sprees, and indulging the children. In short, the "good life."

Then the veneer on that perfect life began to crack. The construction business was booming, and Jeff's hours became long and stressful. A back injury, some painkillers, maybe a little valium, and somehow Jeff became an addict. He unraveled over a period of five years, spending more time at the office and less time with Faith and the kids. Jeff's parents refused to admit their perfect son had a problem. In their eyes, if anything was wrong, it had to be Faith's fault. She had never been good enough for them, not as pretty as their other daughter-in-law.

Faith felt alone, unwanted, miles from her own family, and she worked extremely hard to raise their four children without his help. When Jeff got arrested for possession, it was time for Faith to leave. The world wasn't black and white, or even gray; now it was dismal. If Crayola made "Dismal", what would it look like?

When I met Faith, she had just moved in to the house on my corner. We couldn't believe we'd never met before; it felt like reconnecting with an old friend. Like me, she was a "Yankee" (she from New Jersey, and I from New York), a devoted mother, a lover of books, and a naturally quiet, private person. Also like me, her apparent shyness was a choice, rather than a sign of insecurity. In spite of everything she had been through, Faith remained strong and confident. She felt confident that she'd done the right thing, and confident that somehow, she and the kids would be OK.

Faith was not a talker by nature. She had always expressed herself with her art, but now she had thoughts and emotions too strong to be painted, and too haunting to be left unshared. While she kept up a strong front for the kids, she cried herself to sleep every night. She mourned the man she'd promised to love, for better or for worse, but Jeff was no longer that man. Her kids needed a father, but not one who stole in front of them. Not one who got high in front of them. Not one in jail. The pain had to be washed away before she drowned in it, and I was one of the people there to keep her from getting caught up in the undertow.

For the first time in her life Faith had to live on a real budget. Her father had helped her to buy the house, and Jeff's parents sent child support on his behalf. She accepted the money without groveling or lowering herself in any way. Naturally, her father would help; he loved her. Of course Jeff's wealthy parents supported their grandkids in his absence, even though he himself had no income. She learned to clip coupons and to shop at Goodwill, and she never let her children feel sorry for themselves. They should be grateful for their new home, for their health, and for each other. As for missing "stuff," it was the price they paid for a fresh start.

It was impossible not to love Faith and her surprising combination of nerve, need, sorrow, and optimism. I helped in every way I could, starting with some time for her to heal uninterrupted. Often all four of her kids would trot down to my house with their jammies and spend the night. David would arrive home from work to total chaos, laugh and shake his head. "Again? OK!" He knew I enjoyed their visits as much as they did. They loved him, too, and while they were with us, they had a dad in their life. How full the house seemed, with her four added to my two! How did Faith manage with all of those voices calling for her attention at once?

I loved the kids not only because they were Faith's, but because I found each one unique and inherently irresistible. Aidan, the oldest and the only boy, had taken well to his new role as man of the house. He helped his mother with the yard, and his sisters with homework. Kind, handsome, and athletic, he would surely break hearts one day. The second, Hayley, spoke softly and loved to read. She played on a soccer team, and wrote short stories. Addie, just a year younger, was a real fireball. She told jokes, dressed like a tomboy, and drew incredible pictures, like her mother. They all took special care of the youngest girl, Ella. I tried to as well.

Ella had long, light brown hair and tremendous brown eyes. She loved hugs, stuffed animals, and Polly Pockets. Ella always wanted a long bath before bed, and warm milk with graham crackers. How big and scary the world must have seemed to her, the only one who was allowed to express all of her emotions! She seemed to lighten the burden for the older ones, who bustled about with activities as if nothing of real importance had changed in their lives. All of their anxiety and sadness must have traveled somehow through that sweet little angel, and her siblings comforted her the way they wished they could comfort themselves.

At Christmas I took great delight in finding just the right gifts for each child, like a paint-your-own soccer ball for Hayley, or a special set of drawing pencils for Addie. I would wrap the gifts, put them on the front porch, and do the old "ring the doorbell and run" routine. Once after hearing Faith complain about the huge mess in her minivan, I had her pull up into my driveway. It took almost two hours to sort through mounds of clothing, books, toys, old wrappers, and such, and then clean the inside until it shined. Later that day, I received a thank-you note from the kids. Addie had drawn a picture of a clean back seat, complete with seat belts and sparkles. Little things can mean a lot.

David couldn't believe I had spent my free time cleaning out someone else's vehicle. "Aren't there places that do that sort of thing? Oh yeah, it's called a Car Wash!" he joked.

"Well, it wasn't just for them," I explained. "It was therapeutic. Finding things they'd thought they'd lost, tossing the trash, knowing I was making their lives just a little easier..."

"Hey, don't get me wrong. I'm not mad, but I'm not paying for Caitlin's preschool so that you can clean the neighbor's car all morning. If you need something therapeutic," he teased, glancing around our messy kitchen, "you could try cleaning around here!"

I knew he was kidding; everyone who met Faith wanted to do something nice for her. Other friends appeared with support, advice, casseroles. Each of us had our own special color to add to her life, and she used them to paint her house. The sunroom became a cheerful, sunflower yellow. For the living room, she chose a coordinating orange, which she faux-painted to imitate parchment. For the dining room, wine-red with streaks of midnight blue. Sky blue for the kitchen. Green for the den. All colors of the rainbow for the converted attic, which held bedrooms for her children. Painting said, "There's hope." It said, "You deserve something pretty.' The harder she worked, the faster she healed.

The kids had adjusted, the house looked great. Now she wanted something more: a husband. A husband for herself, a father for her children. Once she made the decision, the question wasn't if, but rather when, she would find him. Two years and over one hundred e-mail correspondents later, Faith met The One. He had enough inner child left to be fun. He rode a motorcycle and taught art at the high school. But he was also financially responsible, handy around the house, a good cook, and a die-hard romantic. He loved Faith, and loved her kids almost as much. He wanted to be a part of their family, and he deserved to be.

They married in one of the most beautiful, pure, outdoor-and-barefoot ceremonies I have ever seen. While this alone could end our story, there's more! Faith's ex-husband successfully completed his rehab, reformed, and remarried. Faith is genuinely happy for him, and even likes his new wife. Her children get to see their father on a regular basis, healthy and drug-free.

With help from her friends, Faith had climbed from Dismal to Happily Ever After, but she deserves most of the credit herself. I've seen many women like Faith refuse to leave Dismal, that murky bottom-of-the-sea where there's no risk of being shocked out of joy and security, because none exist there. These women are afraid to be hurt and unwilling to risk it a second time. Faith's success came from her unwillingness to live without color, beauty, and love—and from her belief that she deserved these things. We don't have to be divorced to learn from this example. Why do so many people settle for comfortably dissatisfying lives when a little risk, or even just a little effort, might change things for the better?

After the wedding, Faith moved away with her children and her new husband. I miss them all terribly. I hadn't realized that what I'd given to them, I'd received back in multiples—in smiles, friendship, and inspiration. It was they who had added color to my life, and not the other way around.

Getting What We Want

Lord Goring: You see, it is a very dangerous thing to listen. If one listens one may be convinced; and a man who allows himself to be convinced by an argument is a thoroughly unreasonable person.

- *An Ideal Husband*, Oscar Wilde

Tina wanted a man who would listen, but she didn't have that. Steven never listened, and was certainly never convinced. He refused to listen to his wife, who begged him to get help for his depression. He was never convinced by his family, who told him that his behavior shocked them and would eventually cost him his marriage, which it did.

The divorce hit Tina hard. Not that it took her by surprise; she was the one who filed. The marriage itself—the sharing of lives, meeting of minds, love, and respect—had been over for years. It was the cold, hard finality of the separation that wrenched her stomach and kept her awake at night. Guilt over whether she had tried hard enough to make it work. Sorrow over dreams of "'til death do us part" smashed like overripe pumpkins run over by a two-ton tractor. That's what Tina felt like: pumpkin guts.

Two years later, we sat on her front porch swing, watching brown leaves dance around the yard in the autumn wind. It had taken about that long for it to sink in that the divorce was not her fault. As the fog lifted from her eyes, she saw the changes in her household since he had left. The kids looked happier. She felt happier. Her daughter was proud of her, and her son didn't talk back any more. Best of all, she felt free! She could go to work, watch her kids, and live her life, free from the overbearing weight of the misery Steven had imposed upon them.

Once she had adjusted, she wanted more. For two years, she had dedicated herself to easing the transition for her children; Steven had never been much help, anyway. She didn't need a man around, but she found that she wanted one. Not just any man, but one who would actually listen to her! She met Marco on a blind date and fell for him right away. They didn't have much in common, but he was gorgeous, flattering, and sensual. She had so much love to give and such a desire to be loved. They had a wildly wonderful romance, until the day it ended.

Tina went from happy to inconsolable. She had always given so much, wasn't it her turn to get what she wanted? I thought so but silently wondered if she'd really lost The Guy, or whether he was just A Guy. Even though she'd been alone for a while, she was still on the rebound. It was like when you go off a strict diet. You head for the chocolate cake and believe it's the most delicious, fabulous food in the world. Then you have a full, healthy meal, and admit that the pasta primavera also tastes good and might sustain you longer than the cake.

Tina wanted cake, but it didn't follow that Marco could provide everything she needed.

I thought about a time I had lost something I desperately wanted. My "Marco" was a house. Just a couple of years earlier, before we had even put our home up for sale, David perused the real estate section in the Sunday paper. We planned to downsize, and he just wanted to get a feel for possibilities. There in black-and-white sat the cutest house we'd ever seen, with "Open House Today" printed right next to the photograph. "I know it's early, but won't it be fun to get some idea of what's out there?" he suggested. "Let's just go and look!"

We pulled up to a cottage so perfect, it practically gleamed in the early spring sun. The bricks were so red, the trim so cleanly white; it was like a Christmas candy cane ready for the taking. Inside we found pristine, hardwood floors, marble countertops in the kitchen, a first-floor master with a small sunroom attached, two perfect bedrooms upstairs for the kids. Everything was brand new. After decades of living in large, old homes with constant renovation expenses, this house promised us easy living and a smaller mortgage. It was five minutes from the kids' schools. I had to have it!

For three days, I thought of nothing else. I fantasized about paint colors. Furniture placement. Morning coffee in the sunroom. Which cabinets would hold the special holiday dishes. How great it would be to park in an attached garage. The street was so quiet. How long would it take us to move in already? I began packing up everything I could, to make our house look clean and clutter-free when we put it on the market.

On the fourth day, the realtor called. He knew I had loved the house, and wanted to let me know an offer had been made.

I became despondent, and then hysterical. I was doing everything right and being punished for it! Here we were on the verge of a national recession, and I was ready to pack up and downsize, no complaints. The candy cane house was my reward for being such a brave, good sport. So how it could it be taken away from me? How cruel a world did we live in? I used an entire box of Kleenex and sobbed 'til my stomach ached. Months of stress came out in tears and heaves until I had nothing left inside but the misery of knowing my perfect house could never belong to me.

Desperately seeking answers, I called my friend Sandy, the wisest woman I know. I explained what had happened and demanded she tell me how the universe could be so cruel. Wasn't I doing everything right? Didn't I deserve the house?

Sandy did not offer the words I had wanted to hear. "It may look like the right house now, but maybe it's not the right house. Maybe you just needed to see that you can find a good house, a smaller house that will meet your needs. Enjoy the feeling of wanting something and knowing that you deserve it. Because you do deserve something great, and when the time comes, you will get it!"

I thanked Sandy, hung up the phone, and started sobbing again. David came in. "Are you OK? What did Sandy say?"

"She doesn't understand!" I yelled. "She's wrong! It is the right house, and I'm losing it! I can't be all wise and philosophical like her; I'm miserable!" I had listened, but I was not convinced. Being convinced would not allow me to wallow, and I desperately needed to wallow.

Five months later, we moved into a different house. It wasn't brand-new, but it had been renovated. It didn't have a sunroom, but it had a finished basement for the kids. It was twenty minutes from school, but the neighborhood had a pool and tennis courts, and lots of children running from yard to yard. "Sandy was right," I admitted to David. "I loved the feeling of, well, wanting that other house so badly. I still think it's a gem; it's just not the right house for us."

I could have told Tina this story. I knew that fundamentally, this man who broke her heart was no different from my candy cane house. I had ignored Sandy not because she was wrong, but because her point of view denied me self-pity and required more strength than I felt I had. Tina would have ignored me for the same reasons. So instead of giving her an earful of wisdom, I just gave her a big hug and a shoulder to cry on. "Let it out," I said. "I know how much it hurts. Let it out, and just know everything is going to get better."

Time healed her wounds, and Tina began to date again. She enjoyed meeting new people, whether or not they had romantic possibilities. Her friend Daniel was one such person. She wasn't physically attracted to him, but that didn't matter: he made her laugh and accepted her without any expectations or criticism. They enjoyed months of cooking together, going to movies, and spending time with her kids without the pressure of dating. They texted and emailed and visited, and then she noticed he had a nice smile. And soulful eyes. And all of a sudden, they became an item.

We don't always get we want, but then again, sometimes we do; we just don't get it right away, or in the form we'd expected. I had wanted a smaller house, and I got a nondescript, beige ranch—you know, like oatmeal—instead of a sparkling candy cane. As it turns out, I love oatmeal! As for Tina, she wanted a man who listened, and she wanted it to be Marco, the sparkling, handsome guy. I've actually never met Daniel, and I certainly would never compare a friend's boyfriend to oatmeal, but I think you see where I'm going with this. I'll just stop while I'm ahead.

A Good Intention Duet

You may not believe this, but I do: when we make mistakes in life, we are presented with opportunities to do better next time. In many ways, that makes the universe a very fair, forgiving, and generous place to live; we get a do-over! It's just like a make-up test in high school, only in high school we receive feedback, on paper, about what we got right and where we messed up. Then we prepare and try again.

In life, there's no quarterly report card. We have to pay close attention or we might not even realize we did something wrong at all. We may not see the end result of our actions, or we may bumble along with good intentions but hurt someone's feelings anyway. Because we tried our best, we think the result must have been unavoidable. In those cases, we may need to feel what it's like to be on the receiving end of such "good intentions" in order to avoid repeating our actions and causing more pain. This is our review session.

But here's the trick: these review sessions come without labels! How are we to recognize invisible placards which we can't even feel as they bonk us on our stubborn heads? Now that I've watched some of my performances on the cosmic

YouTube, I'm worried. I must have missed signs because I've noticed situations repeating. If one time I'm full of good intentions, and the next time I'm hurt by someone professing good intentions, was there something I didn't do right the first time? I hope that sharing these stories with you will wake me like karmic Red Bull and save me a few do-overs in the future.

First Semester: The Hockey Player with Bangles

The first semester of sophomore year, I unpacked into a dream of a house on campus. This made my old dorm room look like a jail cell! There were tall ceilings, large windows, wood floors, and even a fireplace. I'd never met my roommate before, but Jo seemed nice enough. An ice hockey player from New York City, she stood three inches shorter than me, wore faded jeans, and multiple, clanky bangle bracelets. Her straight, jet-black hair framed a cute, freckled face that was almost always smiling.

I really loved living in that house. Everyone was so nice, and we had dinners together on Sunday nights. The only thing that started to grate on me was Jo, and her noisy bracelets. Jo and I kept very different hours, but I was used to that sort of thing. Very few college students like to go to bed early and wake before seven; I knew I was weird that way. I'd fall asleep hours before Jo came home at night, comfortably tucked into my warm bed and dreaming wonderful dreams, and....*clink clink*! Jo came home and got into her pajamas. *Clink clink*! She got into bed. *Clink clink*! All night long she tossed and turned noisily, like a band of kindergartners clanging spoons together.

I mentioned the bracelets a couple of times, and she tried unsuccessfully to remember to take them off before bed. As I became tired and cranky from lack of sleep, every slightly annoying thing Jo did seemed more significant: the snoring, the wet towels on the floor, the friends who showed up past midnight. Then came the final straw. I had just gotten out of the infirmary, having spent five nights of feverish misery away from our beautiful room. Home at last! Then, around 1:00 a.m., I heard giggles and crunches. The women's ice hockey team was celebrating the night's victory with s'mores and roasting the marshmallows at the fireplace in our room!

Wasting no time at all, I spent the next few days frantically looking for a different house for second semester. I had to get away from Jo. Lisa, a woman in my French class, told me her house needed another person and they'd love to have me. I submitted the swap to the housing department and notified my housemates, who were all disappointed. I had spent so much energy avoiding Jo, I hadn't been a very friendly (or present) person to live with, and now I was leaving before they'd gotten a chance to know me, and before I'd really gotten to know them. I felt sad, like I'd missed out on belonging to something great.

Jo found out from the others that I was going to leave. She timidly asked me why, and I said truthfully, "I got a huge single! It's better for me; I go to bed early and I need lots of quiet to study and sleep." But Jo was not stupid.

"It's because of me, isn't it?" she asked.

"No, really, you should see this room I got. I couldn't pass it up."

"It's OK, you can tell me. I want to know."

I sighed heavily. I had really wanted to avoid this. "Well, maybe a little. The bracelet thing, and the messiness, but that night with the hockey team made up my mind. I was so exhausted. I couldn't believe you brought that crowd in."

"We were so quiet!" she countered. "I told them all you were sick and we'd have to be really quiet. No one else has a fireplace!"

"Look, we're not going to agree on this. You're a great girl, I really like you, but we just don't see eye to eye. Please don't take this personally."

She did take it personally, and the last days of the semester weighed heavily on both of us. She felt I had not communicated enough how much her habits bothered me; she could have changed. I resented how guilty she made me feel when I had done everything in my power to avoid hurting her feelings. It was a bad way to part.

Second Semester: The French Connection

The next semester, I moved in with my friend Lisa, from French class, and her friend Laura, who was in the Education program with her. The downstairs of our house held a part-time preschool, and the upstairs had only our bedrooms, plus a small fridge in the hall. The front door was extremely heavy and made of metal; when the safety catch was off, it slammed loudly behind us. The wooden stairs creaked under our feet. It was all part of the charm of living there.

Lisa, Laura, and I had fun together. We all had single bedrooms, but we'd find time to hang out once or twice a week.

About halfway through the semester, I noticed that the other girls had started to come home at the same time more often. A few weeks later, I'd find takeout containers or more sodas than usual in the fridge. Lisa had a car and must have finally started using it. One night when the girls climbed the stairs with a grocery bag each, I said to Lisa, "Oh! I wish I'd known you were going to the store. Can I come next time?"

"Yeah, sure!" she smiled.

But she didn't let me know the next time they were going to the store. Or to the restaurant. Or the next time, or the next. Obviously, I was being left out on purpose. "Are you mad at me?" I asked Lisa. She said no, and we dropped the subject.

Then came the fateful night of "the game." The three of us sat cross-legged on Lisa's floor, sharing a six-pack of Diet Coke and a package of Double-stuff Oreos. Lisa put down her soda and started to gesticulate with her pinkies bent, just like our French professor. I howled with laughter, nearly spitting out my mouthful of Coke. "I know who you are!" Then, so as not to disappoint Laura, who did not take French, she imitated one of their Education professors. "You're a riot!" snorted Laura.

"Wait! Wait! I have another one, one that you both know!" Lisa exclaimed, wiping the crumbs from her lap. "Here, come out into the hall." We obediently got up and followed her. "OK now, watch." She went down the stairs and out the front door. When she reentered the building, she slammed the door as hard as she could. Then she came slowly up the stairs, stomping hard on each stair until she reached the top. I didn't get it. I looked at Laura, but she wouldn't meet my gaze. "You don't know who it is? I'll do it again!" cried Lisa enthusiastically. She went downstairs and repeated the whole thing. I could tell by

Laura's expression that she knew who was being imitated, and that it wasn't her.

The next day I spoke privately with Laura. She told me I'd been driving Lisa nuts all semester, and that's why they'd started going out without me. Lisa couldn't take it anymore, so she tried to make a joke out of it, to let me know in a nice way. It didn't come out nice.

I confronted Lisa. "You really hurt my feelings last night."

Lisa shrugged. "Hey, I was just trying to be funny. You know you make a hell of a lot of noise coming up those stairs."

"Actually, I didn't know."

"Yeah, right! How could you not know? I told you a million times!"

"You did?" I racked my brain but could not recall a single mention of it. "I'm really sorry. I can't believe you let this destroy our friendship. I honestly didn't know!"

Lisa shrugged again. "Look, we're not going to agree on this. You're a great girl, I really like you, but we just don't see eye to eye. Please don't take this personally."

I did take it personally, and the last days of the semester weighed heavily on both of us. I felt she had not communicated enough how much my habits bothered her; I could have changed. She resented how guilty I made her feel when she had done everything in her power to avoid hurting my feelings. It was a bad way to part.

Ava Gardner and the Hobbit

Mabel Chiltern: ...what did you say, Lord Goring, about Mrs. Chevely? Oh! I remember, that she was a genius in the daytime and a beauty at night.

Lady Basildon: What a horrid combination! So very unnatural!

- *An Ideal Husband*, Oscar Wilde

A va turned heads everywhere she went. Every man admired her, and every woman hated her, for her long, wavy hair, exotic, green eyes, and curvy figure. She had an incredible sense of style, too. She always looked classy and elegant without over-doing it. Just the right amount of makeup, just the right accessories, just the right everything. She had already been working at The Company for three years, and she never took vacation. She triple-checked everything she touched, and was up for a promotion. The only thing ostensibly wrong with her was her perky, Valley Girl way of talking. "Y'know, like, y'know, it was like, she was like, he was like, and I was like…" I wanted to smack her.

We met at work in our early twenties. I, who always blended into the background in my discount rack clothes and sensible shoes, avoided her as much as possible. Then fate turned against me: Ava's boss, Dennis Gardner, had accepted a transfer position in another city. Our departments combined, and before long, we were assigned to a joint project. I commiserated with my friends at lunch. "Can you believe it? Stuck with Glamour Girl. Y'know, like, won't this be, y'know, like, fun?"

My misery only increased when I learned she was competent to handle the project without me. I couldn't believe that anyone who talked like that actually had a brain. As it turned out, she was a single-minded, brilliant workaholic who wanted to stay late every night and finish before deadline. She would munch on her celery and hard-boiled egg while perfecting the Power Point; I watched and gobbled down takeout burgers and fries. I felt like a hobbit witness to a wild sorceress. Not even a cute hobbit, but just a short, awkward, simple, chubby, hungry hobbit, minus the hairy feet.

Ava's cubicle had a basket of potpourri in the corner, next to a picture of her with a handsome older man. "So, um, nice photo…" I began, trying to make conversation.

"Yeah, thanks. That's my dad."

"Cool," I said. "Looks like you were on vacation or something?"

"Yeah. That was before he got remarried. We used to, like, do everything together. It was just the two of us when I was growing up." She sighed. "I don't see him that much anymore. Just at the holidays, y'know? It, like, really sucks."

"I'm sorry. That must be hard."

"Yeah." Ava picked up the photo and looked more closely. "He's a lot grayer now, around the temples. But he's still handsome. He was always handsome. My mom passed when I was a kid, and Dad took great care of me. I'm glad he's found someone to keep him company. I mean, like, I'm all grown up now, so I guess it's time." Wow. So she was not the Ice Queen. She looked like a movie star, but she didn't lead a movie star life. No Mom, Dad too busy to call. I had both parents and saw them frequently, but I'd give up some visits to spend just one day of my life looking like her.

She turned back to the screen and began to edit. I pictured myself as her, in a movie but somehow real life. Surreally beautiful, I walk through Paris in a magnificent designer dress that closely hugs my slender but voluptuous body. My long, thick hair cascades around my shoulders and down my back. As I pass the Eiffel Tower, dozens of well-dressed, drop-dead gorgeous French men stare at me, wishing I belonged to them. The scent of my ridiculously expensive perfume catches the wind, drifting its way towards a handsome millionaire. Unable to resist, he quickly buys a dozen red roses, dodges traffic, and presents them to me with a flourish. I snap my gum and smile. "Thanks! That's, like, y'know, really, like, romantic!"

And then, back to reality. No millionaire falls in love with a hobbit wearing TJ Maxx fashions and dime-store cologne. Truth is, if I walked down a Paris street, no one would notice me except to roll their eyes and say, "Ooh-la-la, tacky American!" Anyway, we finished the project in no time, and Ava left on vacation for almost a week. No one knew where she had gone. Nowhere warm, since she had no signs of a tan when she got back.

I hardly spoke to Ava for weeks, though we made the usual small talk at the copier. When she got her promotion, I offered to take her out for a drink to celebrate. Then she took me out for my birthday, and soon enough we had become friends, or at least more than acquaintances. Once I got to know her, she wasn't so intimidating. Though I felt fat and dumpy next to her, she never bragged about her appearance, clothing, or the attention she received from every male in the tristate area. I'd already accepted that Ava had the beauty-and-brains package we hobbits had declared impossible and against all laws of nature; now I got to see her softer side as well.

Her mother passed before Ava's eleventh birthday, and Ava had grown up as Daddy's Little Girl. I couldn't imagine growing up without a mother. No mother to go shopping with, to take you to get your ears pierced, to tuck you in at night. I suppose a father could do some of those things, but it just wouldn't be the same. On top of this, she was an only child. No sister to sit up and giggle with about boys, no big brother to cheer on at basketball games. And now Ava was practically orphaned: her Dad had retired early and moved to Florida with his new wife and her children. He had a whole new family, and she wasn't a part of it. Poor Ava.

During one of our evenings out, Ava told me the truth about her vacation: she had taken time off to have an abortion. She and Dennis had been secretly dating for months. He was older than Ava, and more established in his career. Sophisticated, financially stable, and excessively charming, he reminded her a lot of her father, and she could imagine their future together. Her hopes and the proverbial "test rabbit" died almost simultaneously when he accepted the transfer out of town. She asked him, but he wouldn't go with her to the clinic. Instead she went with a distant cousin, whom she didn't know well and whom she swore to secrecy. She hadn't told her father about any of it, and didn't plan to tell.

"I'm so sorry you had to go through that alone," was all I dared to say.

Ava straightened in her chair and poked at her salad with her fork. "It was OK. I mean, like, it wasn't fun, but I had to do it. What choice did I have? Besides, I'm used to doing things on my own." She put up a brave front, but I had seen the gentle side of Ava and didn't believe for a second that it had been *OK*. I couldn't even imagine being in her position. I couldn't imagine making the choice she did. None of that was OK. It was life-changing and tragic and painful, and that horrible creep, Dennis, had left her like Humpty Dumpty in midair as he plummeted off that wall. Who would put her back together again?

"I wish we'd known each other better then, Ava. I would have taken you. I would have taken care of you. It must have been awful."

"I'm getting over it now. Really. Thanks for letting me get this off my chest. It's been hard not telling anyone, especially with Dennis leaving and all. I miss him so much," she admitted, her eyes filling with tears.

"You miss him?" I croaked unbelievingly. "After he let you go through that all alone? He doesn't deserve to be missed!"

"Don't be so hard on him, Sylvia. You don't know him like I do. He's a wonderful man. Everything I ever wanted, actually:

charming, smart, successful, rich. Besides, there was no way he could come with me even if he wanted to," she continued. "Where would he tell his wife he was going?"

Wife? She's had an affair with a married man? My pity-meter plummeted. Ava should be grateful she just looks like a movie star; she can live in anonymity. Real movie stars always get found out. The public's feverish curiosity overshadows any real consideration of ethics, but somehow holds a power of its own. Strong disapproval could lead to box office death, and so it might nurture a moral rebirth. Ava would have the luxury of recovering outside the public eye, but this also meant she would have no compass to guide her other than her own, and she obviously had no idea which way was north.

I did not know Ava or Dennis well enough to guess what might happen next. She might regret everything and pull herself up with a rope of sincere contrition. She might wallow in misery without ever acknowledging that both adultery and abandonment had occurred. She might even follow him out of town and continue the affair. Regardless, at that moment I felt torn between shocked disappointment and genuine pity. Why go for a married man when thousands of single men would be thrilled to date her? Did she seek him out? Was the attraction really too strong to deny? Was it some sick need for a man like her father?

I kept Ava's secret. My feelings about the entire affair remained tumultuous, but I would not abandon her the way Dennis had. Without me around—like a tabloid reporter ready to strike—Ava would remain in danger of sliding into that seductive, comfortable state of denial that makes repetition all the more likely. How interesting that she hid the truth from her old friends, whose opinions must have mattered more to her. It must have felt safer to tell me; if I had made her feel uncomfortable, she could have cut me loose.

On the other hand, Ava needed all the friends she could get. Rather than making her popular, her "brains and beauty" combination alienated her from most crowds. Men admired her beauty, but only the most arrogant had the nerve to ask her out. Women found so many obvious reasons to be jealous, many didn't bother to get to know her at all. Intellectuals passed her by because she looked like a Barbie doll, but the Barbies didn't have enough to say that interested her. As for me, I'm honestly glad we met. She taught me a lot about life, and relationships, and Power Point. Maybe I taught her a thing or two, or even inspired her to change. She'd probably never had a friend like me before. After seeing what else is out there, I'm sure she realizes now, as I do, that a hobbit is a great thing to be.

Great Expectations:
Donna, Becky and Murray

Ups and downs. Give and take. Mistakes and forgiveness. Relationships can be so complicated!

My marriage to David has already reached the twenty-year mark. We are happier than ever, but I'd be lying if I said all twenty years were perfect. Job issues, kids, the economy, and other bumps in the road have all left their marks. Patience, respect, honesty, and realistic expectations helped us weather these storms. Without these strengths, we may well have ended up like some people we know: dissatisfied and disappointed.

Expecting too much from a partner can lead to discord, but sometimes we expect (and accept) too little. My friend, Donna, expected too much at first, and then too little. Becky always expected too much, so she was never satisfied. Me, I don't expect (or want) very much. But when my needs aren't being met, I have learned to let them be known. Like the Murray incident.

First, meet Donna: charismatic, funny, smart, and very, very loud. Donna came from a large, close-knit, New York, Italian family. I never met them, but I imagine them living in a perpetual Ragu spaghetti sauce commercial. Picture a crowded kitchen. A table in the middle is all but hidden beneath overflowing bowls of spaghetti and meatballs, garlic bread, and salad. Donna, her parents, her brothers and her sisters crowd around, bumping into each other, talking over each other as they pile a little of everything onto their plates. Chaos, love, and parmesan cheese—everywhere. "Buy Ragu! It brings families together!" I'm just taking what I know of Donna and multiplying it by six. I can't be too far off.

There was never a dull moment in the publications office, where Donna kept Cara and me on schedule with military precision. Besides being brunette and under five feet four inches tall, we had nothing in common except an incredible, natural rapport. We ate lunch together, confided in each other, and backed each other up. Everyone called us the Three Little Musketeers.

When Cara and I failed to meet her high expectations, Donna exploded with an expletive-strewn New York attitude that we grew to accept as part of her charm. She always apologized later, and her radiant smile magically healed the battle scars we earned after we'd missed a typo or a revision deadline. In comparison, Cara's sweet country, Southern whispers floated softly like clouds of whipped honey butter. I loved both girls, regardless of decibel and inflection. Our friendship was rare, constant, and true—between the hours of nine and five.

As work friends do, we fell out of touch when I left the company for graduate school. "We're so happy for you!" they told me. Cara followed shortly behind to start a career in computers, and we were "so happy" for her, too. Donna stayed for two more years. She called us on the day she gave notice, thinking it would be fun for the Musketeers to catch up. I couldn't wait to see the girls again and hear what they'd been up to.

Donna and I arrived first. "Hey, so great to see you!" She flashed me an award-winning smile and reached out for a hug. "Cara called. She's got some techie-emergency or something, but she'll be here eventually." She let go of me and took a seat. "I'm glad, actually. There's something I want to tell you both, and I'd almost rather tell you first."

"What is it? Are you OK?"

"I'm moving."

"Yeah…" I prompted her for more. "Like, across-town moving, or out-of-town moving?"

"Out-of-town moving! Far away, because Ethan cheated on me. We're both moving away, together."

Dear Abby,

I just found out my husband of four years has been cheating on me with my maid of honor. They had been dating before our marriage. They slept together the morning of our wedding. They even slept together during our honeymoon (don't ask), and they've been sleeping together ever since. I found out by reading his e-mail. He says he loves only me. What should I do?

Signed, "Deserving What I Got"

"Let me get this straight," I said, brow in a knot of extreme confusion. "Ethan has been having an affair with your maid of honor, and you're moving somewhere together?" Please don't tell me the "other woman" is coming, too! I begged silently.

"OK, now wait and hear me out before you judge him," she said. "It's not his fault! This goes way back, even before I met him. Oh, Sylvie, I'm so flawed! See, I'm just like my Dad. He was always so hard on us growing up, always expecting perfection, and yelling when we messed up. I know I do the same thing. I criticize everybody. I know I've yelled at you, and I'm really, really sorry."

"That's OK, Donna. You never hurt my feelings; sometimes I even thought it was funny." I meant it.

"Really? Thanks so much for saying that. I won't do it again, though, I promise." She blew out hard and tapped her hand on the table. "Let me back up. OK. So, Ethan always knew I was tough on people, including him, but he hoped I would change. He loved me so much, he married me anyway and kept hoping. He'd ask me to chill out, but I never listened. He didn't fold clothes the right way. He didn't balance the checkbook right. I was always on his case about something!" She paused and looked me straight in the eyes. I didn't blink.

"Well, I got what I deserved! I hurt Ethan so much; I drove him into this affair thing. He needed somebody to be nice to him, and it wasn't going to be me. This has all been my fault. The past few months have been hell, but if I could forget the pain, I'd say it was a good thing. I'm in therapy now, and an anger management workshop. I go to yoga three times a week. I feel better than ever—healthier, and more grounded. Ethan has stopped seeing her, for good. So now we're moving to (insert name of remote state here) to start over again. Please be happy for me! Forgive him. I have! I need you to be happy for me."

The next few seconds were unbearable. Strong, independent Donna actually had tears in her eyes. I wanted to say something reassuring, but I was still trying to process what she had just told me. He had been intimate with someone else even on their honeymoon. She's blaming herself for that? She can trust him now? How hard would she deck me if I told her she was being an idiot? Aloud, I said the only words that came to mind: "Donna, if you are happy, then I'm happy for you."

Donna sighed with relief. Cara arrived, and while Donna retold the entire story, I had more time to think. Could Donna's temper really have driven Ethan to adultery? Donna had made Cara cry, but Cara was unusually delicate. Ethan stood six feet tall—a full twelve inches taller than Donna—and had muscles upon muscles. Surely she couldn't frighten him, but I guess she could nag him to death.

I did know one woman as demanding as Donna: Becky. One memorable day, I introduced Becky to my dear friend Tina, who is the cutest kind of ADD possible. You need a road-map to follow Tina's flow of thought, and a bright-red stop sign to get a word in edgewise. She's constantly in a state of minor crisis, loves to vent, and always finds the silver lining in every cloud. An hour with Tina has the same effect as a good cry, a biathlon, a martini, and a Red Bull—all at the same time. And I wouldn't change a thing about her.

The three of us had lunch, Becky, Tina, and I. Tina rambled adorably, as usual, and Becky stayed uncharacteristically silent. As soon as Tina left the table, Becky started in with the criticism, of both Tina and me. Why hadn't I offered to help Tina reorganize her cabinets? Obviously she needed my help, and I didn't even offer. Why did Tina drone on about her problems, and never ask me how I was? Obviously, she's selfish. What kind of friend was I to Tina, leaving her all alone with the cabinet problem, and why did I bother with her, given she was all yack-yack-yack about herself? Obviously this friendship meant nothing to either of us.

How dare she? Becky had told me before that she nagged her husband, but I'd never believed her. Now I was seeing her true colors and wondered why he stayed with her. How could anyone live up to her expectations? And what if they were unreasonable (which they were)? And none of her business! If I were married to Becky, I'd be packing my bags and heading for the door.

Maybe Donna's husband, Ethan, wanted to pack his bags, but instead he had an affair? It's possible, I suppose. Lots of people have them. Maybe some of those people end up back with their spouses. If Donna could actually change, and if Ethan actually gave up the other woman, maybe it could work. I believe in true love, and second chances, and redemption. I decided to be truly happy for Donna, and to wish them well on their new life in that remote state I can't recall.

Anyone can falter, and not just men. I remember years ago feeling that dangerously enticing temptation towards infidelity. Full-time motherhood can be a thankless and lonely job, after all. David had been working a lot lately, and had no patience for my stories about potty disasters. I missed grown-up attention. After tucking Andrew into his crib, I gazed longingly at a picture of the man, not my husband, whom I wished most to see walk in the door. He would take me in his arms, ask me to dance. The only question on my mind was, which Wiggle is cuter: Murray or Greg? I'm sure the Disney Channel could spare one of them for a few weeks of torrid love affair with a bored housewife. I decided on Murray.

"David," I said when he came home that night, "I've decided to run off with Murray Wiggle. He seems like a nice, fun-loving guy, good with kids, plays guitar. What do you think?"

"Murray? Who's he, the red one? I'm much cuter than him." I shot him a look. I wanted a real answer. "I think I need to pay more attention to you," he said, thoughtfully. "I think we need some quality time. I think you need to get out once in a while!" Yes, I did. I had needs that weren't being met, I expressed them, and David listened.

I set realistic expectations. Surely it would be unfair to hit David with the Housewife Blues the second he came in from a hard day at work! I could find other moms to listen to stories he couldn't possibly relate to. Once a month he would watch Andrew so I could have "Girls' Night Out." Twice a month we would hire a sitter and go out, just the two of us, to relax and reconnect. The plan worked well, and I never had to choose between the Wiggles. I wonder if Ethan had ever really tried to communicate with Donna about her unattainable expectations, or whether he just planned to have a good time until he got caught.

That was the last time I ever saw Donna. She moved without sending me her new address, and to be honest, I haven't thought about her much the last few years. OK, the last twelve years. And now that I think about her, the older, wiser me thinks that perhaps we were both optimistic idiots. If Donna fits the general stereotype of a New York-Italian, could Ethan possibly fit the stereotype of tall-gorgeous-tennis-pro? Because if he does, Donna needs to write another letter to Dear Abby:

Dear Abby,

My husband had cheated on me with my former best friend. He blamed it on me, because, after all, it was my fault. I went to therapy and took relaxation classes, and he forgave me. I left my job to go to (insert name of remote state here) and prove to him how wonderful we could be together. Now I've found out he's been sleeping with a dozen or so of his tennis students. Will he ever forgive me for this?

Signed, "Boy, Am I an Idiot"

Seatbelts

I have been saved from injury several times by my seatbelt. I especially remember the day I fainted while driving down the highway. I woke up to crunching sounds as my car repeatedly smacked into concrete barriers on the side of the road. My car was still in motion, my hands gripped the steering wheel, and my seatbelt held me firmly in place. I was pregnant with our first child at the time, and my doctor surmised that the baby had moved into a position that constricted blood flow. Thank heavens for my seatbelt!

Friends are a lot like seat belts. They go everywhere we go: to the mall, out to eat, to the movies. We keep them around all the time, even though we don't usually "need" them. We enjoy their presence and find them reassuring. Those few times when we actually do find ourselves in danger, they hug us close and do their best to take care of us. That's one of the reasons it hurts so much to lose a friend. You rip a hole in your safety net, lose a panel from the quilt that warms you, and silence an instrument in your life's symphony.

I once lost a friend, and it was my fault. Even a mountain of apologies, or a bucketful of tears, couldn't undo my neglect.

There she had lain, alone in a hospital room, no visitors other than her husband. I wasn't there for her. She suffered days of misery with pneumonia, and never even got a card or a call from me. I, who had been her restaurant and shopping buddy for six months, had proven myself a false and shallow friend. Now she wouldn't return my phone calls. She was out of my life forever. Can't say I blame her; some seatbelt I'd turned out to be.

Stacey had experienced this before. Somehow, she always picked the wrong friends, the kind that are fun to be around, but never seem to show up when you need them. I can't believe I ended up in that category. I never meant to! How easy it was to take her for granted. Always giving and never expecting anything in return, always asking how I was and laughing at my bad jokes; she made me feel so comfortable. Our relationship built itself on coffee shops and mall outings, and crumbled on the pointy edge of a hospital visit. I would miss her so much, and all because I failed to be a friend when she really needed one.

I would miss her husband, Glenn, almost as much as Stacey. They had just one car, so I saw him often. Even when we weren't going out as couples, Glenn would drive Stacey over to the mall and walk her to the food court, and we'd visit for a while before parting ways for our girl-time. They were so cute together! "We could afford another car, but then I'd miss my sweetie," he'd coo. She'd blush and smile. A real charmer, Glenn had an adorable face with sparkling blue eyes. He had a great sense of humor, too, just like my old college boyfriend, Craig. I had fallen for Craig the first time I met him. He treated me like an angel, just like Glenn treated Stacey.

Unlike Glenn and Stacey, Craig and I were not meant to be. When I made plans for a junior year abroad, I hoped to make a clean break. I was too young for such a serious relationship, and now we would be separated for more months than we'd been together. Craig wanted to visit me in France, but I told him the expense was too great. When he persisted, I explained my need to learn what I could do all on my own, even if that meant putting our relationship on hold. "You think that now," he said, "but believe me, you'll want me to come. Your friends will forget about you and move on, but I won't. No one loves you like I do. You can't count on anyone but me."

I headed off to France determined to prove him wrong. Unfortunately, my planned, sheltered group experience ended almost as soon as I got there. Long story short, I ended up boarding with a family that didn't like me, attended classes by myself at the local university, and proved too shy and awkward for the French students to bother noticing. I quickly became lonely and homesick. Once a week, I called my family. At first I also wrote letters to my college friends, but none of them wrote back. Everything Craig warned me about had come true, and I had been wrong to think independence would automatically be fun.

Life is so much better when you have someone to share it with! Craig bought a plane ticket, and we traveled to Italy together. He proposed in Venice, in a gondola under the Bridge of Sighs. I would never have to feel lonely again. Hollywood magic came to life: handsome hero spends all of his savings to travel across the Atlantic to woo his one true love. But before you get caught up in it, tell me how I should have answered his proposal. Remember, he had insisted all of my friends would abandon me. Is that kind? He proposed to me at my weakest, when I'd never felt more alone. Could he be sure I truly loved him, or was it simply the best time to get the answer he wanted?

When I replay our relationship in my head, I am astonished at how many times Craig had either raised me up so high that I felt insecure and unworthy of the praise, or cut me down so low that I felt I didn't deserve anyone's love at all. My friends thought our relationship was ideal, but it was an ideal that reality could only imitate. That made his adoration cinematic, empty, desperate, suffocating, and almost frightening. I'm glad I didn't marry him. It would have destroyed me.

As I mentioned, Glenn and Craig had a lot in common. They were adorable and charismatic, and especially loved caring for the women in their lives. So when Stacey caught a bad cold, I didn't worry. I figured she'd spend a few days at home, with Glenn waiting on her hand and foot, and call me when she felt better. She didn't answer her cell phone, so eventually I called Glenn on his. "Oh, she'll be fine. Just give her a few more days," he told me the first time. "Well, she has been in the hospital the last few days," he let slip the second time.

"In the hospital? Oh no! What's wrong? Is she okay? Can she have visitors?"

"Don't worry; she's fine! Just a little pneumonia. She gets it every couple of years. They're just keeping her for observation. She's really not up for visitors, but I'll tell her you called," he promised.

"What hospital is she in? Can I send her a card? I know she's allergic to flowers. Balloons, maybe? Can I talk to her?"

"She's sleeping now. I'm sure she'll get out soon, like maybe even tomorrow. Why don't you send a card to the house, and I'll bring it to her? Or she'll get it at home, probably, because she's almost better. I'll have her call you when she's rested up a bit. Bye!"

Relieved, I sent a card to the house and waited to hear from one of them. I called and left messages on both of their cells and their home phone. No response. Luckily, I ran into Stacey at the grocery a few weeks later. "Stacey! I'm so thrilled to see you! I've been worried. How are you feeling?" I reached out to hug her, but she stepped away, cold as ice. "I'm sorry," I said, surprised. "Are you still feeling fragile? Are you contagious, or something?"

"No, I'm not contagious," she spit back. "Figures that's all you're worried about. Glenn told me, and he's right: you can tell who your *true* friends are when they don't show up. You didn't show up, Sylvia. Not even a card. Just forget it. Just forget you saw me."

"But I did send a card! And I kept calling! I didn't even know you were in the hospital until you were practically out. Didn't Glenn tell you I called?"

"Yeah, right. Nice try. I was in there for a week. No visitors. No cards. No calls. I was just out of sight, out of mind to you. That seemed to be working, so don't fix it." The glare in her eyes revealed fury but also pain—pain and disappointment, or maybe even a little hatred. She turned on her heel and walked away, refusing to stop as I called her name. It was the last time I ever saw her.

It could have been me. If I had married Craig, I could have been Stacey. He was the type who might have withheld information, erased phone messages, and thrown away cards to prove to me that I was alone in the world without him. Maybe he'd been dumped before and vowed never to let it happen again. Maybe he picked me because I wasn't strong or independent yet. With him, I never would have been.

Sometimes when I'm upset or sad, my husband hands me the phone and tells me to ring my oldest friend: no jealousy, no hesitation, just wanting the best for me. I love him for that. "Go ahead and call Julie. You'll feel better." If I had married Craig, there would be no Julies.

Stacey meant a lot to me, but she'll never know. Now I understand why she always talked about friends in the past tense: Glenn cut her seat belts every time they tried to tighten. She couldn't possibly feel safe that way, but that's what he wanted. They shared a single car so that he would always be in charge of her; he would always know where she was and who she was with. That left just the two of them, so devoted and loving, seemingly the perfect couple. He was all she had in the world, and he had seen to that.

Renovations
(by HGTV and Oscar Wilde)

My favorite television channel by far is HGTV. I love watching old homes being restored, worn-out fixtures and furniture getting a second chance at life. Why tear things down or throw them away when some ingenuity, carpentry, sweat, paint, and fabric can make them beautiful again? Of course very few people have the skill—and the vision, and the time, and the money—to work such miracles, but it is refreshing and satisfying to see those ridiculously good-looking and unusually talented reality stars accomplish magical home transformations during a half-hour show.

David and I share a deep appreciation of old architecture. We have restored two homes, and let me tell you, a half-hour segment could not begin to tell the story! In both cases, the first renovations were the most expensive and the least television-worthy: pipes and wiring. Later updates were infinitely more fun (cosmetic), and every once in a while, small miracles occurred. Once David noticed a boarded-up area on the outside of our house that was hidden from the inside. We hired a carpenter to open the wall, and he uncovered a stained glass window that some previous owner had not wanted. Imagine covering something so beautiful! Now, that was worthy of HGTV.

Not everyone is up for that sort of challenge. Why buy an old house that needs work, when a suburban tract-home is available move-in ready? I get it, really. It's a choice. If only the attitude ended with housing, I wouldn't have a problem with it, but it doesn't. There's a laziness in today's society, a reluctance to work on things if an easy way out can be found. Why keep the old house that requires work? Why keep up an old relationship that requires work? Truth is, many old homes have a beauty that can't be matched by newer ones. Many old relationships have a beauty that can't be matched by newer ones. History cannot be created with a fast-forward or rewind button on the remote.

Relationships, like houses, may become a little weary after a while, but that doesn't mean it's time to move on: it's just time for HGTV. For example, pipes and wiring may need some tending. To me, they represent communication. Next, cosmetic improvements. To me, they represent the fun: outings, shared interests, a little spice to remind you of why you were attracted in the first place. Renovations take time and effort, and sadly, not every relationship can (or should) be saved. If the foundation is solid, you've got a chance. But sometimes all you can do is cut your losses and leave.

Gertrude and Bobbie had been together for over fifteen years. They met right after college, in a local softball league. Bobbie had always known she preferred women, but Trudy (Gertrude) had always dated men. Nevertheless, it was love at first sight, on both sides. They bought a tidy little house around the corner from mine, adopted a dog, and began a lovely, quiet life together.

Trudy and I met by chance in the neighborhood. Bobbie worked odd hours at the hospital so I never got to meet her. It must have been hard keeping a relationship going, living with different schedules the way they did, but Trudy never complained. She seemed like a very patient and caring person, always looking on the bright side, and I was glad to have found a new friend. We got together regularly to walk the dogs and talk about life.

Years flew by, leaving many changes in their wake. My friend and neighbor Faith married and moved away, Jana's husband relocated them to California; Tina got divorced; and Kristen moved with her family to Hawaii. Thank heaven for Trudy and our Saturday morning walks! The only other constants in our neighborhood seemed to be the street signs and the hundred-year-old houses we passed. It was reassuring to an old-fashioned girl like me that at least those houses remained the same, regardless of the upheaval of their inhabitants.

One Saturday morning, I learned that even Trudy's life was not as steady as I'd come to believe. Bobbie never listened to her anymore, had even stopped asking about her day. She had become obsessively plugged in, spending every free moment on the computer, apparently oblivious to the fact that Trudy had begun to wither in loneliness. "At this point, we're just roommates," Trudy confided in me. "It's like I don't count anymore. We never go out. Bobbie won't even come to my family functions. She's so wrapped up in herself and that stupid screen."

"Please tell me this is new," I replied. "Surely you haven't been living like this for long. Can you snap her out of it?"

"Well, it came on gradually. I'm not even sure when it started. A few years ago, maybe," she admitted. "I tell her we have a problem, but she always denies it! She says she still loves me, but I don't feel it. Who is she now? She used to be so colorful, and now she's a dull, gray person lounging around in dull, gray sweatpants all the time. I feel so alone."

In my gut, I feared the worst. You can't renovate a relationship solo, and Bobbie did not seem willing to participate. Selfishly, I did not want to see any more upheaval among my friends. No more divorces, no more moving away! I felt empty and out of place, like one of those houses we always passed, frozen in time while everything changed around me.

Bobbie was shocked when Trudy left. She pleaded for Trudy to stay and begged for a second chance. In Trudy's opinion, Bobbie had blown a hundred second chances. Trudy would never be sure whether she'd tried hard enough to be heard, or whether she'd simply stayed too long in an impossible situation. Had she been whiny, or a victim of neglect? Either way, it was too late now. The frayed wiring had ignited, the house was on fire, and it was time to vacate. Trudy moved across town and tried to make a new life for herself.

As sad as I was to see her ago, I supported Trudy's decision. How awful it must be to feel lonely in your own home! To beg and plead for attention from someone who promised to love you forever! I've watched my divorced friends suffer in unhappy relationships. Most of them eventually found happiness, whether alone or with someone new. I wished hard and long for Trudy's happiness, whatever form that might take. Truth is, as much as we loved our 1904 fixer-upper, when the recession hit, David and I had to face reality and move to a suburban tract home. Sometimes you have no choice but to move on.

Almost a year later, I was happily surprised to see Trudy and another woman walking down the street. The woman wore stylish jeans and a bright-red sweater, and smiled at Trudy with a look that said, "You can do no wrong in my eyes." Wow, I thought to myself. Trudy found herself someone new already; good for her! Trudy greeted me with a big hug and introduced her companion: "Sylvia, meet Bobbie!"

The allegorical house fire had woken Bobbie out of her computer-induced stupor. After a fire, of course, there is only one thing to do: renovate! Fix the wiring, repaint the walls. Bobbie started by finding a therapist, who helped her to understand how she had been hiding from the world by losing herself in screens. That was hard to face. Then, though she doubted she could ever regain Trudy's esteem, she put the laptop away, joined a hiking group, reconnected with old friends, and bought some new clothes. When Trudy ran into her weeks later, she was shocked to see Bobbie's transformation.

Soon after, they tentatively reunited. Bobbie apologized to Trudy for all of the times she hadn't listened or participated in life. She had been so out of touch, so far in denial, that she simply hadn't seen what now appeared so painfully obvious. Trudy finally had a chance to be heard, but she also gave Bobbie a chance to redeem herself by showing how much she had changed. They forgave each other, reminisced about the good times, and planned for the future together.

The best part of restoring their relationship was regaining the beauty of what had been there all along, hidden behind months (or even years) of problems. Like David and I had discovered the stained glass behind our dining room wall, Bobbie and Trudy rediscovered the essence of their love and, finding it intact, vowed never to take advantage of it or lose sight of it again. I've seen many women find love a second time, but this was the first time I'd seen a couple so happily reunited.

It may be easy to fall in love, but keeping love alive requires work. It took tremendous courage, as well as redemption and forgiveness, for my friends to overcome the divide that had grown between them. For this reason, I gave these real people the names of characters from one of my favorite plays: *An Ideal Husband*, by Oscar Wilde. The triumph of the Chilterns' marriage in the play reminds me so much of what Trudy and Bobbie achieved.

> *Lady Chiltern: You were to me something apart from common life, a thing pure, noble, honest, without stain. The world seemed to me finer because you were in it, and goodness more real because you lived.....*
>
> *Sir Robert Chiltern: There was your mistake...It is not the perfect, but the imperfect who have need of love.*

Sir Robert has fallen in his wife's esteem, but redeems himself in a sincere and significant manner, and thus Lady Chiltern forgives him. Likewise, my friend Trudy forgave Bobbie when she redeemed herself by facing her weaknesses and conquering them. Together they share a gusto for life and a commitment to each other that few people ever experience. I toast both couples, the real and the fictional: Thank you for providing new inspiration for even such a romantic as myself. To your happiness!

> *Sir Robert: (taking her hand): Gertrude, is it love you feel for me, or is it pity merely?*

Lady Chiltern: (kisses him): It is love, Robert. Love, and only love. For both of us a new life is beginning.

—An Ideal Husband, Oscar Wilde

MOTHERHOOD

MOTHERHOOD

One thing about motherhood: you can always do better. In school, you get an A and say proudly, "I did it." At work, you get a raise or promotion and say, "Good for me!" With motherhood, the job is never done and the evaluation period is endless. Someone is always doing better than you: neater house, better-behaved children, more involved in the PTA. Across from us once lived a family in which both parents were doctors. Mrs. Doctor also gardens, sews and bakes. "Wow," Andrew told me on the way home from school one fall afternoon. "Kate's mom made the most incredible cookies for the bake sale! And Kate said her mom's making her a Guinevere costume for Halloween, with real silk and everything."

"Yeah, she's amazing!" parroted Caitlin. "She can do everything! Of course, so can you. We wouldn't love you if you couldn't do things as good as she can." I shot her a look which would have made Attila the Hun cry like a baby. Andrew panicked, glared at Caitlin and stuck his elbow in her ribs. "Oh! I mean, we love you no matter what, Mom!"

These superwomen really get my goat. Kids never compare you to the moms who skip all the field trips, or who can't be bothered to bring their kids to yet another birthday extravaganza at Chaos-R-Us party center. They compare you to Mrs. Claus, Taylor Swift, or Mrs. Doctor. I don't bake from scratch, OK? I can't sew or take out an appendix. But I love to go to the zoo, the park, the bowling alley. I help them with homework, read stories, toss a ball in the backyard, and let them know they're loved.

Those simple moments may be the ones they hold onto forever. The things they will tell their own children. And once again, you don't know when, how or why the wonderful things will happen. The magic is the work involved in creating the scene for the wonderful things, and the everyday efforts we make adding up to our children's happiness, hoping to mold our children into adults who see the silver lining in every cloud. And I wouldn't be any better at it if I could take out an appendix.

One essential for success at motherhood must be good intentions. First we try to give our kids what we would have wanted, because we know what that is. When our kids start to show preferences, we try to give them what they want. When we realize that they want either too much or the "wrong" things altogether, we kick ourselves for being too indulgent or not instructive enough. If we protect them too much, they never learn. If we give them too much freedom, they get hurt. When we throw up our hands in despair, unable to be the perfect mothers they deserve, we can always fall back on, "We meant well."

Motherhood provides a focus that changes us completely. When things go wrong at work, we have no time to stew: we have to grin through homework. When the car breaks down, we can't call our friends to whine: we call other moms, for help with carpool. When snow blocks our driveway, we don't complain about shoveling: we find boots and mittens, and build snowmen.

We are no longer the center of our own lives. In fact, sometimes we get lost in the equation! While we excel at taking care of others, we often forget to take care of ourselves. So accustomed to helping, we even rush to the aid of other adults when they appear to need us, and yet we forget that when we feel overwhelmed, we can ask for help, too. Sometimes we look back at our own early experiences hoping they will provide guidance, even though the world is now so different from the one we grew up in.

The stories that follow include various themes, including standing up for ourselves, and, of course, protecting our little ones. Motherhood can be so scary! Scary, humbling, and magical. Sometimes it's hard for me to believe that people ride roller coasters because they actually enjoy the experience, the thrill of the surprise bends and dips, ups and downs. As for me, I get motion sick backing out of the driveway. But the Motherhood Roller Coaster is well worth the fear and nausea. My medications of choice to get me through include perspective, friendship, and gratitude, along with healthy doses of laughter and fun. Our children won't be little for long. Carpe diem! Seize the day!

Wonton Soup Hero

Like all mothers and daughters, Mom and I are incredibly similar yet couldn't be more different. She grew up in small-town Connecticut and raised me in an affluent New York suburb. Like her mother, she was friendly and adorable and the life of the party, while I was bookish and shy. She ran a choir and directed shows; I sat in a corner of the living room with my guitar and a pen, transforming my often beautiful poetry into melodically snore-inducing songs. I moved south then north, then south, then north again, and she is still living within an hour of her birthplace.

Even so, we're like twins. We were both athletic children who gave up our baseball gloves when we discovered boys. Our hearts soar in unison upon hearing all types of old music, from Antonio Vivaldi's "Four Seasons" violin concertos, to "Sherry" by Frankie Valli and the Four Seasons. We both enjoy books and antiquing, and a nice view of nature from an air-conditioned hotel room. We do major "damage" when let loose in a shopping mall with Dad's credit card, and we're both consistently running late wherever we go.

Looking back at how many doors I slammed during my adolescence, I'm lucky she still speaks to me at all. When I was fourteen, I had chicken pox for almost two weeks. I walked around the house with a towel over my head so that no one could see my speckled face. Certainly it was the most traumatic thing in my whole entire life, and no one should have to look at me. I bellowed, sobbed, stomped, and moped. Medusa could be no more frightening than Sylvie with the Pox. Watching me bump into walls and almost fall down the basement stairs, Mom made the sensible suggestion that I remove the towel. Brave, brave woman! I choose to forget my reaction to her advice. She saved me from falling down those stairs, though, that's for sure.

My mother has saved me, time and again, from falling down stairs. Usually I fought against each suggestion, constantly trying to assert my independence and deny that the platitude is true: Mothers Know Best. One August afternoon, however, I finally admitted that even when a girl is old enough to vote, Mom may have a better understanding of the candidates.

The two of us sat miserably in a Chinese restaurant, sipping on wonton soup and staring in opposite directions. In a few weeks I would be returning for my senior year in college. This should have been a fun outing, one of a few last hurrahs before returning to a full schedule of challenging courses and senior seminars. I was engaged to a young man who worshipped me, and while we hadn't set a date yet, we were nearly grown-up, married people. Mom didn't approve. Oh, she liked him well enough, but she didn't think I should marry him. Mothers always think they know best, but she lived her life, and it was time for me to live mine. We weren't talking to one another.

My only respite from Mom was my summer job as a camp counselor, five glorious days a week. When I was little, I'd loved camp more than anything; working as a counselor confirmed to me that other than Walt Disney World, camp is The Happiest Place on Earth. My group had fifteen girls aged eight to ten years old, each with a strong personality, each trying to be grown up and independent in a new environment. Shawna, a tall, shy, freckled girl with an Australian accent, arrived at camp clinging to her school friend Emily. Emily had jet-black hair, extremely large ears and tremendous buck teeth. For some reason, the "popular girls" (yes, it does start that young) took a liking to Emily, and poor Shawna had to fly solo after the first week.

At first Shawna came crying to me; she felt so hurt and alone. I sat down with her and Emily, and soon they exchanged hugs and promises to sit together every lunch. For the rest of the day, making new friends would be OK, part of the camp experience. Shawna did make new friends (though tentatively, at first) and enjoyed all of the camp activities more because of it. The popular girls never accepted Shawna, but Emily (bless her) kept her word and sat with her at lunch. I wondered what would happen when these two old friends returned to school in the fall; likely, they would go separate ways. It was sad, but all part of growing up.

I knew too well the emotions Shawna must have been feeling: jealousy, pain, and fear of rejection. Watching this truly beautiful child wade through so much emotional muck, I felt proud of her, and confident that she would come out the other side sparkling-clean and stronger from the experience. As for Emily, part of me wanted to take her by the toes, hang her upside down for a while, and lecture her: "Can you see straight now? You dumped this wonderful friend for shallow social-climbers who will peak at eighteen, go through multiple husbands, and spend all of their alimony on hair salons and plastic surgery!"

On the other hand, the irony that the truly plain-looking girl had been elevated, above her stunning friend, to "cool" status, had not been lost on me. Maybe the universe knew what it was doing.

Camp meant more to me than a summer job. It represented a world that I desperately wanted to be a part of, namely any one that involved kids. I'd mentioned this desire to Mom once: "I've always loved camp so much; maybe I could work at a camp after graduation. You know, like in the business office or something."

"I understand you love kids," Mom replied, "but that's not practical. Besides, nine months of the year, all they do is marketing. You'd only get to be with the kids in the summer, and how often would they stop into the office? You'll be too old to be a counselor soon."

Fine. Just rip my heart out without letting me give it a try. "Well, I could be an elementary school teacher, then. All year long, I could be with kids, and then I could work summers at a camp or something."

"Believe me, honey, it's not as much fun as you'd think. Remember, I taught music in the public school system. Not every school is as great as the one you had; some are pretty scary. You could end up with thirty-six wild kids who won't sit down or pay attention, and then you've got parents, administrators, and red-tape to magnify your developing migraine. You're so smart! You can do anything. Just set your sights a little higher."

Once again, she thought she knew better than me. Just because she burned out after teaching for a while doesn't mean I would. Who says anything is higher than teaching? I thought that was supposed to be one of the noblest professions! When she says I can do anything, she means anything that warrants her approval.

As the summer wore on, I became more determined to be my own person. One academic year stood between me and complete freedom! I could work at a camp if I wanted to; she couldn't stop me. I could marry Craig if I wanted to; she couldn't stop me. Of course, Craig didn't want me to work with kids, either, or even to raise our own. He told me all about his fantasy of our future. He pictured himself staying at home with our children. I'd pull up at 6:30 p.m. every evening in a shiny, black limo, exhausted from my high-powered executive job in the big city. He'd help me into my robe and slippers, make me a martini, and serve me magnificent, home-cooked meals. I'd pat the kids on the head, and he'd go read them bedtime stories while I soaked in a hot tub.

Obviously, neither of the people whose love and support I counted on most had any clue of who I was or what I wanted. I was surprised Mom didn't approve of Craig, given how similar their hopes were for my career. I'd marry him anyway, because I could, and because I'd promised to, and because Mom was not going to tell me what to do with my life. Then I'd tell Craig that if anyone was going to stay home with our future kids, it would be me. So there! Look how well Shawna found her way; she became an independent little person right before my eyes, and she was only ten. Well, I could fend for myself, too, if Mom would just let me make my own decisions! Once I was married, she'd have to give up and let me alone.

So there we were on a Saturday afternoon, Mom and I, giving each other the silent treatment at the Chinese restaurant. Head down, I stared at my soup. Mom stared at the top of my head. Silence. *Slurp*. Silence. *Slurp*. Then Mom broke the silence. "My friend Lillian's son is home for the summer."

"That's nice."

"He broke up with his girlfriend. Lillian didn't like her, anyway. She hopes he'll find someone nice while he's home."

"Mmm-hmmm," I mumbled, cutting a won ton with the edge of my spoon.

"He's working in construction for the summer, but he's premed, you know. Very smart, polite boy. You might like him."

"Mom! I told you already. I'm engaged."

"Yeah, that's right. You're engaged."

Yes, I was engaged. Of course, I'd had doubts. Everyone has doubts; people call them cold feet. He'd never introduced me to his family or friends. I didn't even have a ring yet. But you can't sneak out on a blind date with a pre-med just because you have cold feet. So what if Craig's hopes and dreams would crush mine? He loved me. We would make it work.

Mom sat there a long time, restless and frustrated. Finally she cried out, "Why are you doing this? You don't have to do this!" A flood of tears rushed out of me, obscuring my view of the soup I had hardly tasted anyway. I looked into her eyes for the first time in months. "Help me, Mom! I don't want to marry him! Help me get out of it!" And Mom got me out of it the way only a mother can. She truly saved me.

I thanked her; I know I did. I thanked her, went back to school, and the course of my life had been altered for the better. Onward. It's amazing how close we can come to disaster and once it has passed, bury the memory of it like a tin can in the back garden. We step on top of it, water over it, plant around it, knowing all the while that one day a shovel may unexpectedly unearth it; but we desperately hope it won't. Although we buried the incident and never brought it up again, our relationship had changed forever that day. I had learned an invaluable lesson: as much as I wanted to deny it, mothers often do know best.

I'll never know whether I would have been happy working in a camp or a school. Mom had been right about the boy; maybe she was right about my career. I tried business, and law, and business again, and eventually landed the best job in the world when I became a mother, myself. One year, with Mother's Day approaching, I spent almost an hour searching the drugstore racks for a card that was sweet but not too sappy to send. Finally, the right card presented itself. In a flowery, Hallmark kind of way, it declared this simple truth: we can never truly appreciate our mothers until we become mothers ourselves. We never understand how much we are loved, until we love another with that selfless passion that a parent feels. We never understand the joy of sacrifice until we put aside our own careers, hobbies, desires, purchases, and preferences to provide a loving, secure, comfortable environment for our offspring.

That day in the Chinese restaurant, Mom's heart was breaking as much as mine. She had spent half of her life doing her best to make my life everything it could be. While I feared spending my future in an unhappy marriage, she had seen others actually do just that. How could she let me make that mistake, when she could prevent it from happening? There are mistakes that children must be allowed to make in order to learn from them; it's part of growing up. But there are also train wrecks we should save them from, especially when they are willing to shout, "It's too much! Save me!" Sometimes the lesson isn't about the mistake but that it's okay to admit we've messed up, that we need help, that we need…Mom.

It's actually much easier to save our children than to let them fall, or fail, on their own. Because it's less painful for us, we fool ourselves that we always act in their best interest. For a while we have to protect them, keep our toddlers from running into the road, for example. But then we have to let go. If we protect them too much, they'll never be confident, capable adults; that's why the mother birds push the baby birds out of the nest. I'm only learning now, after years of mothering experience, to let my children make their own decisions, whether or not I agree with them. I let them handle their own interpersonal issues without acting as an intermediary. I think they are stronger because of it. However, I would never refuse a call for help if they cried, even silently, "It's too much! Save me!"

My daughter and I are already alike and different. She takes everything literally; I live in metaphor. She asserts her independence; I couldn't until I approached thirty. On the other hand, we both love to close the blinds and dance in the living room. We both love Taylor Swift, parades, fairy stories, and The Princess Diaries movies. I will have many opportunities to offer advice, applause, and a shoulder to cry on, and with luck, we will never have to confront each other over lunch at a Chinese restaurant. If we do, I hope to save the day, like my mom, my wonton soup hero.

Parades and Sandpits

Here comes the sun, here comes the sun

And I say, "It's all right"

- *"Here Comes the Sun,"* by George Harrison, The Beatles

Ever have "one of those days?" Sometimes no matter how hard we try, we let those days get to us. We try to smile but a cloud hovers watchfully, blocking out the sun whenever an opportunity arises. I always try to look on the bright side. So that lovely spring day, when I waited four hours for a repairman who never showed up, I made the best of it. In fact, I was determined to make that day so productive, the rest of my week would pass in total leisure. I mopped the floors, dusted the furniture, scrubbed the tub, baked a dozen large muffins, and ran a couple of loads of laundry.

I was "in the zone" and so engrossed with my housework that I lost track of time. I had to be at school by 2:00 p.m. for the annual celebration of the Kentucky Derby. We had lived through years of preschool and lower-school Derby events—nine years of them, in fact. Nine years of shoebox parade floats, theme hats made at home, races on yardstick horses. The first few years, I squirmed my way to the front of the mob of parents with camcorders. I waved, cheered my child's class as they passed, grinned so hard my cheeks hurt. "Aren't they adorable? Oh, this is so cute!" The next few years, I grumbled a little about getting the float done but took dozens of snapshots. These last years, well, at least I remember to bring my camera.

Please understand, it is only normal to become jaded after a while. And today of all days, I had done so well not getting upset about the repairman. My tub sparkled! Another hour or two and the entire house would be immaculate. But no, I had to race off for yet another K-2 parade. Cloud over my head again. Which part of the day would win out: waiting for yet another repairman who didn't show and didn't call, scrubbing grout 'til half my nail polish was worn off, or attending a ninth year of "Aren't they adorable?"

The school parking lot looked like the mall on Black Friday. Don't people have anything better to do than go to these events? It seems every time you blink, there is another reason to show up at the school. Not only are there parades, but also band concerts, plays, parties, and field trips. I was a pretty good sport, all things considered. I'd handed out more cupcakes, chaperoned more trips to the zoo, and collated more homework packets than most of the moms I knew. But it seemed like every single mother, father, and grandparent had packed themselves into the parking lot today.

I arrived just a few minutes before the event, in time to watch the car in front of me take the last available space. Could this day get any worse? A visiting grandmother waved to me encouragingly as she pulled aside a rake from the corner of the parking lot, just beyond the pavement. "I guess you can park here," she said. "After all, there are no spaces left." The day was saved! Gratefully I called out my thanks and drove into a sandy area by the edge of the grass. My front tires immediately began to sink. I tried to back out, but the more my wheels spun, the deeper I became entrenched. I had pulled into the track-team's practice sand pit!

Of course this would happen today. I should have stayed at home, cleaning. Why did I have to be here miserable, late, and stuck in the sand? Frustrated with myself and the situation, I heard someone with a bullhorn make a welcome announcement. Racing towards the front of the school, I dialed AAA on my cell-phone. They would arrive within forty-five minutes, right about the time when all of these cars would be trying to pull out of the parking lot. Figures.

I grumped over to find my daughter, who looked adorable in her *Butterfly Meadow* derby hat. The second grade all wore book-themed hats; first graders were draped in paper jockey "silks"; and the kindergartners would race paper and yardstick horses down the school driveway. Unfortunately I was stuck almost behind the start of the parade, so I caught only a fleeting glimpse of each group as they walked away from me down the parent-lined driveway. Smart kids. I'd walk away from me, too, given my foul mood.

Many parents had brought camcorders. They were cheering and smiling the way I used to cheer and smile. I looked especially at the kindergarten parents. Was this their first derby? They certainly seemed to be enjoying themselves. One glance at the kids' faces assured me that just about everyone, except for me, thought this was as exciting as the Macy's Thanksgiving

Day Parade. What was I missing? Anything but the right attitude? When had I become a Derby Scrooge?

The tow truck waited for most of the crowd to disperse, and then eased my car out. So much sand had gotten into the undercarriage, the driver hauled the car off to my repair shop. David was away on business, but surely I could find someone to take me and the kids home. A glance confirmed that one last family remained, packing up their vehicle. The Bartons have three boys and a very large van—room to spare! I didn't know them well, but I did know they live on the same side of town. "Is your car OK?" Jane Barton asked. "Do you need a lift?" I gratefully accepted the offer, gathered my kids from the school office, and climbed up into the van.

I'm not always comfortable inviting people into my home at a moment's notice. (While we live comfortably with a certain level of mess, the whole world doesn't need to know that.) Today, however, my house sparkled and smelled faintly of chocolate chip muffins. When we pulled into the driveway, I invited everyone in without hesitation. The kids gobbled down their muffins and ran down to the basement, where they played the rest of the afternoon. That very weekend, both of my kids asked to see the Bartons again, all three boys! And they did.

That magical afternoon, I learned the value of sandpits and late repairmen. Had my car not gotten stuck, these new friendships may never have been formed. Had the repairman showed up, I would have had neither a clean home nor fresh muffins for our impromptu play date. How often do extraordinary gifts masquerade as unfortunate events? I wondered: had I not allowed myself to get upset about the sandpit, would I have enjoyed watching the parade?

"Caitlin," I said, as I thoughtfully wiped down the counter, "I was just thinking about the parade at school today. Did you have fun?"

"Of course, Mommy! I got to be in a big parade. How could it not be wonderful?" Indeed. There's perspective. How could it not?

"You know, Mom," piped in Andrew, "I was just thinking: it turned out to be a good thing that your car got stuck. We made new friends!"

How did my children learn this lesson so quickly and painlessly? Well, they are children, after all. They didn't have to fret over time stuck at home or the upcoming $135 bill from the service station.

Then again, I didn't have to fret, either. Worry and whining didn't change a thing; they just prevented me from enjoying a beautiful afternoon at the school. Instead of getting frustrated at every turn, I could have just enjoyed the moment and waited to see what would happen next. If a genuine, certified, magic genie appeared and said, "I will find your children some terrific new friends, guaranteed. Just give me $135," I would gladly hand the money over. Money well spent, if you ask me.

Parades and sandpits: equally wonderful.

Perspective

Being a carpool mom means you're constantly meeting new people: school moms, chess tournament moms, karate moms, art class moms, camp moms, tennis moms. Occasionally even a dad, but mostly other moms. They will be your companions one hour every Friday for six weeks, or maybe eight hours one Saturday per month. You don't choose them, but you also may never see them again. It is a strange, comfortable routine of meet-and-greet, and sometimes I am happy to just sit on the sidelines and watch the stories unfold.

In our culture of jeans and SUVs, most activity-moms are friendly and approachable. You can identify the nicest women right away, as well as the whiners, the joiners, and the name-droppers. They're all fine for an hour a time, but there was once a woman I couldn't spend an hour with. Everything about her was tight. She wore her hair slicked back into a tight, neat bun. She had thin, tight lips. Her clothes were tight on her tall, skinny frame. She carried herself tightly, perfect posture, choppy movements. When I overheard her speaking, she was always complaining. Even her name sounded tight to me: Katrina.

"Chelsea's teacher says she doodles in her notebook," Katrina was explaining to another mom. "I told Chelsea that school is important. Notebooks are part of school. But did she listen? No! I had to buy her a new notebook. I made her copy everything from the old book into the new one, and she had to pay me back the dollar. At some point, she's gotta learn." For the record, Chelsea was seven-years-old.

I couldn't bear to listen, so I made my excuses to the group and ran off for the hour. At some point, she's gotta learn? My heart was pounding with indignation. Good grief, woman: put things in perspective! Doodles are creative. Maybe the kid is a budding artist. What kind of crazy mother would make her daughter recopy everything? The stress I felt sharpened my senses uncomfortably. My throat tightened; I couldn't breathe. I had to get out of there, right away.

The bright sun hurt my eyes as I reached the parking lot, but at least the fresh air soothed my nerves a bit. I knew of only one antidote to my anger, something that would help me forget Katrina, and it wasn't pretty. My mother would understand; I think it's genetic. It's deeply ingrained in our DNA, and we call it hunting. My car practically drove itself; it knew where to take me. Determined and focused, I entered the automatic sliding door, grabbed a cart, and headed for girls' clothing.

I located the one item I really needed, my version of the rare White Rhino: a long-sleeved, white button-down shirt for Caitlin to wear with her Hermione Granger Halloween costume. One left in her size, and it was on sale! Every molecule of my body relaxed, as if I'd just enjoyed a 90-minute Swedish massage. The memory of Katrina was now a million miles away. Smiling with the satisfaction of the hunt, I placed the shirt in my otherwise-empty cart and headed toward the cashier. My friend Margaret greeted me just past checkout, at the in-store Starbucks. "Hi, Sylvie," she smiled. "My son is at play rehearsal; I've got half an hour. Wanna sit?"

"Sure, I've got a few minutes," I replied, checking my watch. "Get anything good?"

"Nah. I've been desperately looking for plastic Native Americans to put in my kid's diorama. In the old days, there were "cowboy and Indian" sets. I give up! I got these half-naked World Wide Wrestlers and some brown felt to cover their... whatever it is they're wearing. It's the best I can do."

"I hear you!" I commiserated. Neither of us are good at crafts. We see the words To Do at Home and break out in hives. The level of agitation depends on whether the kid wants to do it without help, and what the other parents in the class do. I'll never forget my own report on cows' stomachs in the sixth grade. The other kids came in with 3-D digestive systems. One was made with plastic bottles strung together and suspended from a wire frame. Another had made-to-scale paper mache stomachs that opened on the sides to reveal descriptions of each part. Mine was a multi-color diagram on poster-board, and I got a C minus. I hated my parents that day.

We found a table and sat down with our frappuccinos. "Tonight's going to be rough," Margaret complained. "My son missed two days of school last week, and they gave him fifteen sheets of make-up work, due tomorrow! We don't have time for that. Schools are so worried now about meeting goals, they're overdoing it on the little stuff."

"I hear you," I said, blood pressure rising again. "Moms, too. It's all about perspective! This woman I just met jumped all over her seven-year-old for doodling in her notebook."

Margaret had just read Amy Chua's *Battle Hymn of a Tiger Mother*, while I had Wendy Mogel's *The Blessing of a B Minus* stuffed into my purse. We were bursting at the seams with opinions, talking over each other in complete agreement.

Margaret quickly summarized *Battle Hymn*: Amy Chua strictly disciplined her children in order to help them reach their potential and to prepare them for success in the competitive world environment. A grade of A minus was unacceptable at the Chua home. Play dates and other American customs were sacrificial lambs when it came to child-rearing winners, and eventually her grateful children excelled and thanked her. At the end of the book, Ms. Chua tempers her position with a warning not to overdo, but the media hype leaves that part out. I bet lots of people never read that far.

Blessings of a B Minus happened to hit my radar at about the same time. Wendy Mogel, a clinical psychologist, has seen many adolescents crumble under the pressure that society, peers, and, often, parents, place upon them. She recommends balance, love, consistency, and acceptance. Her philosophy is drizzled all over with Jewish wisdom. Reading her book reassured me that my adolescent son's behavior was not only normal, but also a necessary part of his becoming an independent adult. Now that I had provided Andrew with a supportive and nurturing childhood, it was time to sit back and let him fly a little, with rules, Band-Aids, and earplugs handy.

Margaret and I couldn't achieve Tiger Mother status even if we wanted to; we just don't have it in us. Neither of us excels at discipline, nor do we want our children to fear us, and we both come from comfortable backgrounds. While some parents who can afford luxuries for their children also push them to extremes, others simply spoil them rotten without giving them any direction or reason to apply themselves. It is easy to say, "give up your lucrative career and sell hand-woven beer cozies if that is your true desire" when you have a trust fund. Some children of wealthy, busy parents often receive everything they could ever want, and so nothing thrills them.

"It's all a question of context and perspective," concluded Margaret as she sucked down the last of her Cinnamon Dolce, "and whether you're willing to sacrifice joy in childhood for security or motivation later. I'm not sure that pushing a kid will necessarily lead to happiness or success."

"Couldn't agree with you more!" I declared emphatically, tossing my empty cup away. "Sorry, I've gotta run, or I'll be late for pick-up." I gave her a quick hug and dashed out to my car.

With camaraderie, adrenalin, and caffeine coursing through my veins, I arrived with three minutes to spare. The waiting room now swarmed with people: moms for pick-up, and new arrivals with kids in tow for the next session. I pushed my way towards a far corner so that Caitlin would see me when she emerged from the door. There sat Katrina, straight as an arrow in her chair and looking severely constipated. Her eyes kept flitting back and forth across the room, but she appeared fixated on a young boy about ten years old. The boy wandered from woman to woman, patting their hair and hugging them. Then he walked over to me, and gave me a pat and a hug. "I'm sorry," Katrina apologized, pulling him away. "I guess he likes you. This is Topher."

"Oh, that's okay. I'm glad!" I smiled at her son. "Nice to meet you, Topher. I like you, too."

Over the next few weeks, I watched Katrina as she hurried her daughter in at the last minute, always with Topher.

He required constant supervision. Katrina couldn't dash off to Target for frappuccinos and scholarly debates about child-rearing; she was too busy with real life! I couldn't even imagine spending a day in her shoes. How high-and-mighty we can be when we have no clue what other people are living with. I felt ashamed of my Starbucks tirade, all pumped up on Cinnamon Dolce. Don't get me wrong: I still feel bad for Chelsea and her notebook situation. But it makes sense now, and the person without proper perspective had turned out to be me.

Katrina had grown up always doing the "right thing," working hard, and excelling. She had always been rewarded for staying on the straight-and-narrow. Then Topher arrived and turned her world upside-down. He could not fit in with other children. He could not control himself, and she could not control him. She had to control whatever she could, so that the floor didn't fall out from under her feet.

I can't imagine my daughter in Chelsea's shoes, either—or rather, I refuse to imagine it. In many ways, Chelsea is blessed. Her parents are kind and love her very much. She lives in a pretty house, attends a good school, and participates in activities like other children. Facing facts, though, her sweet but needy older brother requires much more attention than she does. Because she is capable, and because her mother requires it of her, Chelsea will learn to do the "right thing." She will follow the rules, work hard, and excel, just like her mother. Her reward may be unclear. Success will mean she requires less attention, but I hope that's not what she gets.

According to U.S. Centers for Disease Control and Prevention, one in 110 children live with some form of autism. We meet these children all the time, and we meet their parents. Some parents meet the challenge so well, they deserve medals of honor. I'm humbled by their accomplishments, and ashamed of judging anyone from my comfortable, complacent seat of ignorance. Margaret and I fretted over Halloween costumes and dioramas, while women like Katrina worry about getting through the day. We deliberated between frappuccino flavors while Katrina kept her watchful eyes on a child who couldn't ever be "dropped off" anywhere.

It's inspiring to see Katrina's strength, resilience, and courage, even the little that I get to see them, one hour every Friday for six weeks, or even briefly in the parking lot. Carpool moms can learn as much from sitting around reception areas, as from debating trends and bestsellers while safely sipping lattes. We can live without caffeine, but a little perspective goes a long way.

What They Don't Know

"What they don't know can't hurt them," people always say. How absurd! Of course it can. In *Pride and Prejudice*, when Elizabeth learns that her youngest sister, Lydia, has eloped with the undeserving Mr. Wickham, she bemoans the fact that she withheld knowledge of his character from her family.

> *When I consider...that I might have prevented it! I who knew what he was. ...*
>
> *Had his character been known, this could not have happened.*

Knowledge can be a powerful thing. Lydia Bennet may very well have ignored her sister's admonitions, had she made any, but then again, she may not. What we know for certain is that Elizabeth suffered more cruelly because she remained silent. Had she spoken and the same fate occurred, at least she would have felt she had done what she could. We all want to protect those we love, to the extent that we can and to the extent that they let us.

People have told me I'm a little bit overprotective. Not a lot, but a little. After all, I did let Andrew spend two weeks at computer camp in Chicago, but I waited until he was twelve to send him. I do take both kids to karate, but I wouldn't sign Caitlin up for the weapons session. I make them wear shoes when they go outside. I tell them to bring jackets if I think they might get cold. When they forget an instrument or a homework assignment, I drive all the way back to school to drop it off for them. Heaven forbid they should live with the consequences of having left it at home!

My parents weren't overprotective, but they raised me in another dimension called the Twentieth Century. In that far-away place, seat belts were optional, as were bike helmets. I left the house Saturday morning to go play "nearby," and just had to be home in time for supper. There were no cell phones, but I had a quarter stuck in my shoe for emergencies. When I missed the morning bus, my mom didn't drive me once I was old enough to walk. Certainly if I left an assignment at home, it would stay there 'til I claimed it, if it hadn't already been thrown away.

I turned thirteen a few days before a family vacation to the Poconos. Teenager at last! How liberating it felt. No longer stuck with the little kids! I was on my way to real life. My sister would spend her time at the lodge in the "Children's Lounge," while I got to ice skate, compete in trivia contests, and go to disco parties with the teenagers. We'd never stayed at a resort like that, where the kids run free of their parents from morning 'til night. This would be the best vacation ever.

The kids at the resort came from all over – all over New York and Connecticut, anyway. I immediately fell head-over-heels for a preppy boy from Connecticut named Sandy. He wore Izod shirts—the ones with the little alligators—tucked in, with a woven leather belt. He looked so grown up, I swooned. Sandy thought of me as a friend and let me tag along with him and a hoodlum named Michael from Long Island, who in turn had a huge crush on me. The three of us went tobogganing and ice skating, watched TV in the lounge, and scarfed enough pizza and chips to make the average kid sick. It felt like heaven, except of course that Sandy wasn't interested in me, and I wasn't interested in Michael. What a pathetic triangle of unrequited teenage puppy love.

Enter Jason, a slick-talking Long Islander with feathered hair and satin shirts, very "Saturday Night Fever." But after all, it *was* 1979. He saw me dancing with my triangle boys, and asked whether I'd enter the dance contest with him (couples only). Of course I agreed. Jason was sixteen, very confident, and he could boogie with the best of them. There were two days before the contest, so we started working on a routine right away.

Jason thought Sandy was a nerd and Michael was a dweeb. I only had a few days invested in them, so I didn't spend much time considering it. I still couldn't believe a sixteen-year-old boy had asked me to dance with him! He was so handsome. I didn't like his parents, though. I met them that night when Jason stopped at their room to get a sweater. They had friends with them, and an open cooler of beer. Empty cans littered the desk, and the room reeked of cigarettes, or something else people smoke. "Hey, kids! We're just having some beers. Jason, want one? Offer one to your little friend here." We declined, but I don't know if Jason would have taken one if I hadn't been with him.

Just before the contest, we stopped again at Jason's room for his sweater. I didn't suspect a thing, but when he closed the door, he kissed me. At first it was okay, but then things began to heat up. Soon I felt like I was in danger. I went rigid with fear. "What's wrong?" he asked. "You're not in the mood? Are you a virgin or something? How old are you, anyway?"

Of course I'm a virgin, you jerk! I wanted to scream. Instead I played it cool, and lied. "I'm fourteen, and a half. It's OK. I'm just really nervous about the contest. Aren't you nervous? It starts in an hour. Can't we go run the routine one more time?"

"Oh yeah, sure. You're right; we don't have much time now. That's cool," he answered, running a comb through his hair and sneaking a peek at himself in the mirror. "Yeah. Let's go back and run the routine."

We won the dance contest. What a thrill! My trophy stood eighteen inches high, the tallest one I'd ever received. I couldn't wait to show my parents. For the moment, though, I felt more agitated than celebratory. I put the trophy down and went to the refreshment table, silently planning how to avoid Jason for the rest of the night. Two Diet Cokes later, I noticed Michael and Sandy looking at me. I smiled and headed in their direction, but they turned and walked out of the room. "Hey, wait up!" I called. I followed them out the door and down the hall.

"Congrats on the contest," Michael said as I caught up to them.

"Thanks. Hey, you guys wanna hang out?"

Sandy and Michael exchanged glances. "No, we're cool. Go back to your boyfriend."

"He's not my boyfriend!" I protested. "Come on. It's my last night!"

"Whatever. Look, when Jason showed up, you totally dumped us. We're going to the arcade. You go back to your party and play Dancing Queen or whatever."

I walked numbly back to get my trophy. I had been such a jerk. No wonder the guys didn't want to hang out with me anymore! I blew it, and all for some conceited octopus. The trophy was not where I left it; someone had decided to take it home as a souvenir. The room was full of people, but I had no one to talk to. Jason was slow-dancing with some girl who looked at least sixteen, so at least I didn't have to worry about him anymore. He hadn't cared about me after all! He just wanted me to help him win the contest. What if he hadn't stopped pawing me when I wanted him to? What if something horrible had happened, and then he went off with another girl?

Reality came crashing down on me, and I ran out of the room, sobbing. I had nothing to show for this, my first week of almost-adulthood, except an invisible dunce cap. I had chosen a guy who looked cool over friends who really liked me. I had been offered beer by sleazy adults, and had practically been molested by their sleazy son. My beautiful trophy had been stolen. I wondered what my sister had done all week in the children's program. Maybe crafts and board games weren't so bad after all. Maybe growing up could wait a while.

When I look back now and think what could have happened to me that week, at a time when things were "safe" for young people, I forgive myself for being just a little overprotective now. I was such a good kid! I never shoplifted, cheated on a test, or tried marijuana. Other kids did, but I was never even tempted. Maybe that's why the universe protected me that night from Jason the Octopus. Or maybe I was just lucky. I don't want to take any chances with Caitlin, never take the risk of being unlucky. I don't want to let her out of my sight until she's twenty-one, though I know I will have to.

David and I joke that Andrew can start dating at fifteen, and Caitlin at thirty-five. For now, I'm so glad she's safe and innocent. We've still got years of crafts and board games ahead of us. I know that there is a danger in being too innocent, too sure of others' good intentions. I'd rather she learn about some things through my own stories of near-disaster than through experiences of her own.

"What they don't know" can hurt them. One day I will tell Caitlin about the Poconos. She should know what can hurt her, and then choose her own path. Lydia Bennet may have chosen to ignore Elizabeth, had she spoken. But Lydia's mother always indulged and never instructed.

Not just in the Bennets' time but even a generation ago, women weren't free to discuss such things with their daughters. Now that we are, how do we begin? It's a delicate balance, and there's no script appropriate for all children to hear. Perhaps the most important thing isn't just what we say when we sit down for the "big" talks, but the messages we dole out over the years when we think they're not listening, the examples we set when we think they're not watching. Then we let them know our doors are always open. Open doors. Listening and watching. Them to us, and us to them.

A Dog for Dana

Dana's family had reached capacity. It had two working parents, two cars, two kids, and a nanny. Then everything changed.

Now, every family is different and reaches capacity at different points. I know families with one parent, two parents, four involved grandparents, no involved grandparents, no children, only children, four children, eight children—all of them at their natural capacity. You just have to find the right balance, working with the resources you have, to create a comfortable life without too many nervous breakdowns or over-the-top sacrifices that end in tears or screaming matches.

Dana and I met years ago at the playground, just after she quit her accounting job. She was so put together! So spiffy! So...obviously new to the full-time mom thing. She actually wore makeup, a clean shirt, and pants without elastic! What a riot. I liked her anyway, and she told me her story.

Dana had been determined to have it all. Six weeks after giving birth to Joe Junior (her second child), she returned to the office as if nothing in her life had changed. Over the next couple of months she'd grown pale, weak, and thin. She couldn't keep any food down. A visit to a specialist allayed her fears: she was simply suffering from SMS: "SuperMom Syndrome." There actually is such a thing! Why isn't there a telethon for that?

Of course it didn't help that her husband, Joseph Sr., had become accustomed to life BC (before children). In the years BC, Joe worked longer hours than Dana, so she took care of everything in the house. He expected that to continue, even after the children started coming. SuperMom Syndrome helped Dana accept the fact she could not do it all. Joe Senior never offered to pitch in, so her job would have to go.

Of course since the job was gone, the nanny had to go, too. Dana found herself alone in new territory, and the first few weeks almost scared her back to a desk job. How could she clip Joey's nails without snipping the skin on his tiny fingers? She put socks on his hands instead, so he wouldn't scratch himself, and waited 'til the next trip to the pediatrician. Her sister's vet cut her dog's nails; wouldn't the doctor do the same thing for the baby? Turned out he would, and he did.

A professional through and through, Dana devoted herself to becoming a competent, full-time Mom. She read every parenting book ever written, jarred her own baby food, and played the baby Mozart CDs as he fell asleep. She learned how to bake cookies from scratch and get Elmer's Glue off the antique furniture. Joe Senior liked having her at home. She was Queen of the Castle, in charge of everything! But in real life, queens have an entire staff of helpers to make their lives easier. Now that she understood what it was all about, poor Dana developed a new respect for stay-at-home mothers.

Then the most incredible thing happened: Joey was ready for kindergarten. Free at last! Or at least, until noon. The more independent Joey got, the more life returned closer to what it had been BC. Dana got to shower. Dana met friends for coffee. Dana even read books that didn't begin with "once upon a time"! Those few hours a day meant everything to her. She found herself again, and by doing so, rediscovered her own importance not just as a mom, but as a person in her own right.

Everyone in Joey's kindergarten class seemed to have a pet, and soon Joey was clamoring for a puppy. Joe Senior thought it was a great idea. Their daughter Lucy, a boisterous third-grader, wanted a girl dog to name Lucinda of Waverly Place, and Joey wanted a boy dog to name Pikachu. Joe Sr. decided that Dana should pick out the puppies, and that he himself would name them. Santa would bring each child a puppy for Christmas.

Dana brought me along to visit a breeder, for advice and moral support. Opening a baby gate, we knelt down to watch a heap of adorable, squirming lab puppies crawl all over each other. "You will be happy with the labs," smiled the breeder. "They are perfect with kids. Loyal, energetic, and so playful. Aren't they adorable?" Dana smiled methodically and said that yes, they were the cutest things she'd ever seen.

Back in the car, I asked Dana what was wrong. She did not seem as excited about the lab puppies in person as she had been on the drive out to see them. "Well," she began, "they are certainly very cute. But they're just babies with tails. You know what they are? They're more work for me! I'm finally free from diapers. They're potty training all over again. They'll mess on the rug. Guess who will have to clean it up? They'll chew on the furniture, rip up Joe's slippers, and he'll blame me for getting the puppies. The kids won't take care of them. Sure, they say they will, but they won't." She sighed deeply. "But...it will make the kids so happy, and Joe Senior said to get the puppies for Christmas..."

"Hey, Dana," I interrupted. "Stop for a minute! What do *you* want? This sounds like a really big commitment. Do you want puppies? What would make you happy?"

She smiled quietly. "Now that the house is going to be empty more and more? Now that the kids don't need me as much as they used to?" The wheels were churning. "I know what I don't want. I don't want more work. I don't want pee stains on the carpet, or screams about chewed-up Barbie dolls. I don't want to spend more time taking care of things that don't belong to me. I guess what I really want is something that's mine! If I'm going to take care of something else, I want to get something out of it. I want a dog for me."

On the drive home we stopped off at the Humane Society. We skipped the puppies and went straight to the adult dogs. Older, house-trained, good companion dogs. A few weeks later, Dana drove home with a big ol' middle-aged mutt in the back of the station wagon. She invited me over to meet the new member of the family.

Mia was almost indescribable. Her coat was brown and black and grey, as if she just couldn't make up her mind what color to wear. She was shaggy in some areas and wiry in others. Her ears went up and then fell over in flaps, and I recognized every breed and no breed at all in her features. She had big deep eyes that made my heart melt, and she'd come over and put her head in Dana's lap while we drank our coffee. She didn't snap when the kids yanked her tail, and she dutifully fetched every stick they threw in the backyard. After all the playing, she came back in and lay down at Dana's feet.

Dana leaned down to pet her. "You're such a good dog, yes you are!" she crooned. "Mia is everything I could have asked for," she told me. "Of all the dogs we looked at, I knew I'd have to go back and take her home. She had the perfect name. Do you know what her name means? It means mine. A dog for me. She is mine."

I was proud of Dana for choosing Mia over the lab puppies. I was even a little proud of the small part I played in the choice, simply by asking Dana what she wanted. Joe Senior hadn't done that. Dana hadn't done it for herself. Truth be told, I often don't do that for myself. I wish someone would help with the dishes, but I don't ask my husband to do it. I bet he would. I wish I could soak in a hot tub for a while, or curl up with a good book, but I don't make it a priority in my day.

Families reach capacity. Moms reach capacity, too. Before we explode, or implode, or wither or sigh or cry, we should look in the mirror and ask, "Who's taking care of me?" The reflection looking back at us should reply, "What are you waiting for?"

Let Them Dream

"**O**h, Mom! Why, oh why? This is terrible!!!"

Megan, my friend Pamela's precocious daughter, ran past me with a desperate, pleading look in her eyes. "Pardon me, Mrs. Forrest, I don't mean to interrupt, but this is *extremely* important."

"Oh, I understand," I replied, quickly removing myself from the kitchen. Megan only had two settings (Asleep and Drama-Queen), so I was not actually concerned. If anything had been really wrong, we would have known. Heck, all the neighbors would have heard the screams by now. I eaves dropped from the living room.

"Why what, Sweetness?" Pamela asked calmly.

"Why hasn't anything fantastic happened to me yet? I mean, I'm almost eight and a half years old, and my life is just so ordinary!"

Pamela and I were quietly amused. Our generation grew up watching the Brady Bunch. We were *bred* for ordinary! For us, it was exciting enough to see Jan disguise herself while shopping for freckle remover. We had crushes on Greg or Peter, or simply wished we could be part of that wonderful, playful, ordinary family. In short, we had low expectations for outrageous things happening to normal people, and normal life did not seem the least bit disappointing. How marvelous! We grew up easy to please.

Not so today's generation. They have very few media examples of "ordinary", so only extraordinary appears natural or acceptable to them. Megan and my daughter Caitlin watch shows about a girl with a top web show, a boy band coming from obscurity into stardom, and a school on a cruise ship. No wonder they feel disappointed! Poor Megan sings her heart out along with the newest Taylor Swift CD, and no agent has coming knocking on the door to sign her. How can she get discovered? How long will it take? After all, she's almost eight-*and-a-half*-years-old!

Unlike Megan, my Caitlin shuns the spotlight. She has been dancing for five years, but doesn't want anyone at school to know. She chose not to sign up for the spring recital two years in a row, and did not even audition for a part in The Nutcracker. Almost all of her dance friends did, but Caitlin didn't want to give up her art class or her opportunity to play with friends on the weekend. I think that's great! Better than great: I think it's Brady-level normal! Why should a little girl be put under the pressure of night-time rehearsals, demands of perfection, and thousands of strange eyes peering at them? Why shouldn't she rather play outside with her neighborhood friends than spend Saturday afternoons sitting in a back room waiting for her thirty seconds in the spotlight?

I would be thrilled for Caitlin to truly embrace "ordinary." Certainly most people grow up to have ordinary lives, no matter how many thrilling TV programs, movies, and video games they are exposed to in their youth. A peek at the tabloids, and what parent would want their kid to be a star? So many child stars end up on drugs, or washed up at sixteen. If life hits its zenith before you're old enough to vote, that's a lot of years of free-fall misery.

"You have so much, Megan!" Pamela assured her. "You have a nice home, lots of people who love you, and all sorts of activities. Maybe we shouldn't watch any more television. It gives you unrealistic expectations about everyday life. Let's just enjoy your time as a little girl."

"But, Mom! That girl on TV has her own video and she's only seven years old. And I'm *not* a little girl! I just told you: I'm almost eight *and a half*!" It would be no consolation for her to hear that she is a big star to Pamela.

Don't get me wrong: I do believe in dreaming. Children's literature and movies are filled with stories of ordinary kids who find out that they are actually magic, or demigods, or royalty. They can ride dragons, or shrink to the size of a popsicle, or save the world. Fantasy is healthy and fun. I would never discourage such wonderful dreams. Still, there is something fabulously unpressured about "ordinary" that just might hold a key to happiness.

I had a pretty ordinary dream when I was that age. While other kids dreamt of being astronauts, firefighters, doctors, ballerinas, or baseball stars, I wanted to be an elementary school teacher. Maybe, after years of teaching, I'd become an elementary school principal. Yes! That would be the pinnacle for me: principal. First I'd become a great teacher, one that always smiled and made children happy to learn. Then one day I'd run a school. Everyone would want to go to my school because it would be the best one for miles around. Years later my students would come back and say, "Do you remember me? You were the best principal ever!"

You may be surprised that no one encouraged this dream of mine. My generation of girls was the first to be allowed to dream big, bigger than the old triad of choices for professional women: nurse, secretary, teacher. "Don't you want to be a lawyer, like your father?" people would say. "Or a business woman. You could be an executive and work in a big office tower in the city." And worst of all: "Don't teach. Only people who can't *do*, teach."

I allowed all of these voices to sway me. Teaching would not be a viable option. I tried law school but left after a year. I tried business but found it boring and unfulfilling. Out of desperation, I finally got my Masters in Business Administration, hoping that a higher-level position would make the business world more satisfying. A top company hired me into management. My parents were so proud! I had my own office, a high salary, and a new, professional wardrobe.

During lunch hour, I hid at my desk and wistfully perused the Help Wanted section, circling anything that mentioned education, publishing, or children. My son said his first word to a nanny, because I wasn't at home with him: I was off fulfilling a dream I never wanted.

Now I live a new dream: full-time mom. This would never have hit my radar when I was growing up. Not with Aretha demanding R-E-S-P-E-C-T on the radio. Motherhood was a bogus profession that had been forced upon women because men wanted to keep them in the kitchen! A whole generation of women had persevered, picketed, and protested so that I could make the same salary as any man. I'm grateful for those women, but completely unashamed to tell them, "Thanks, but no thanks!"

Many of my peers also left careers for motherhood. I thought I was alone, but soon articles abounded on the trend of well-educated, professional women choosing home over office. I had spent years trying to fit myself into someone else's vision of happiness. I would never talk anyone out of their dreams. I understand the cost.

Returning to Pamela's kitchen, Megan continued to unburden her woes on her mother. "We were *gonna* have a band, but Jenna says she's afraid sing in public and Tara only wants to sing songs that I don't even know. This is a disaster. A total, *complete* disaster!"

How I wanted to laugh! This beautiful, talented, tiny girl was afraid that her dream would never become true because she had run into obstacles before she hit double-digits. She will have so many dreams in the years to come, many of which will change, and none of which will guarantee happiness.

"Oh, sweetheart," Pamela crooned. "You just keep practicing on your own, as much as you want. When the time is right, you'll find the right girls for your band."

"I will? Do you really think I will, Mom?" Megan sniffed.

"Sure, sweetie." She handed her daughter a Kleenex.

"You know, Mom," Megan began, thoughtfully twisting her tissue, "while I'm not being a big pop star, I could be a fashion designer. I'm really good at art, and I love fashion."

"Yes, you could, Megan! You'd be great at that. That sounds great."

One day my daughter may yearn for the spotlight, like her friend Megan. She may not. My dream for her is only that she'll find her joy—be it onstage, in front of a classroom, in a courtroom, or changing diapers. Her joy will come from her dreams, not mine, and I hope that she will not let anyone tell her what those dreams should be. I wrote this for her:

Feel free to dream big. Feel free to dream small.

I'll be there to catch you whenever you fall.

If your goal is attainable, one day you'll reach it.

If not, find another and try to achieve it.

Your dreams seem to change with your mood, and I'm betting

That the fun is in "wanting" as much as in "getting."

You feel safe to dream (at least in small part)

'Cause you know that I love you, with all of my heart.

Giving Too Much

J en is the kind of mother that you always wish you'd had, and the kind of mom I'd always wished I could be. She handled the three Cs (cooking, cleaning, carpool) with incredible grace and patience, as if someone was paying her a million-dollar salary to do these things. Or like she starred on some reality show called "The Perfect Mother," with cameras following her around everywhere she went, or like the universe stuck her here on earth to provide the rest of us moms with a reminder of how much we still have to learn.

Also a perfect wife, Jen didn't complain once when her husband's business led them into financial distress during the recession. She stood by her man as he chose to keep the family business going without laying off employees. They even pulled their kids out of Catholic school in order to keep the books balanced until the economy turned around. As long as the family was together and healthy, Jen would never complain.

I met Jen in a homeschool group. We found each other immediately, having so much in common. Like her, I had a soft-hearted husband who had sacrificed to keep a business going.

Like her, I'd always had faith that everything would work out for the best.

In truth, for my family, it really had. We'd had to downsize, but I loved our new, smaller home. Cleaning house took half the time, lost shoes and backpacks appeared twice as fast, and the heating bill was now a faint blip on the radar. We were now always in each other's way, but at least that meant we were always in each other's presence. I hadn't realized it until the move, but we had been drifting as far apart as space allowed. Every square foot we lost has become a gift of a new moment together.

Jen enjoyed homeschooling, but admitted she'd begun to resent Mark's business. At first she was all for making sacrifices so he didn't have lay off employees. Then she saw that time and time again, Mark essentially chose the needs of these strangers over the needs of his own family. They didn't have to take their kids out of school. They didn't have to cut back on household expenses. She did so that they didn't have to. But this wasn't charity; charity would be OK. This was about choice.

Now this I could relate to. While I was truly happy in our new home, our family had sacrificed in order to keep our business afloat. We had the burden of a personal guarantee on a lease, empty offices, no work coming in, and employees that expected their weekly paycheck no matter what. We received no thank-yous from most of them, no acknowledgement of the fact we'd put our home up for sale.

Eventually even David got tired of giving. He wanted a thank-you. He started to get angry. "Don't be angry at these people," I told him. "They're never going to thank you. It's not who they are. Just make different choices! If you want to get a thank you, give to your family. We will thank you. *I* will thank you. If you give to these people, only do it because you truly want to, or you'll be disappointed. If you still choose to do it, I won't complain."

Noble sentiments, indeed, but I did start complaining, and for the same reason Jen did. At some point, you choose your family! Your family, for heaven's sake!

David's business finally picked up again. So did Mark's, and Jen's children went back to Catholic school. Jen had given up so much during the previous year, she was thrilled to have some quiet time again. She read, baked, sewed, and kept her house as neat as a pin. She began to think about volunteer opportunities, or maybe even taking an art class. Then her eldest son asked to return to homeschool.

"What could I say?" she asked rhetorically. "Tim doesn't feel like he fits in anymore. Middle school is tough, we all know that. Of course I told him it was fine to come back home." Tim was just about my Andrew's age—almost thirteen—so Jen figured she'd still have some time to herself. It wouldn't be like having the little ones underfoot; she could run out to the store and leave Tim by himself for an hour or two. In fact, a few months into the school year, Tim encouraged her to sign up for that pottery class she'd been pining for. "Such a great mom deserves a treat," he had told her.

How she loved it! Once a week, for two hours at a stretch, she became simply *Jen* and not *Mom*, living just for herself for a brief shining period. She cleared her mind of everything but the spin of the wheel and the feel of the soft clay in her fingers. It became meditative, making up for every vacation she hadn't taken, every night she'd sat up with a sick child while Mark slept soundly.

Weeks later, Jen came over for coffee. Tim and Andrew ran down to the basement to play video games and Jen took her usual seat at my kitchen table. "Can I share something with you?" she asked softly, eyes to the basement door. Concerned, I nodded and leaned in. "I had to quit my ceramics class."

"What happened?" I asked, surprised. "Too expensive?"

"No, it's not that. It's, well, I don't know why this is so upsetting." She put her mug down and crossed her hands over her heart. "I just feel so violated." I feared the worst but said nothing. "It's Tim. He's been lying to me! When I was going to class each week, he told me he was getting his assignments done, but he wasn't. He played video games, watched You-Tube—who knows what else–but he didn't do his schoolwork. He looked me straight in the eye and lied to me, every Wednesday. Lie, lie, lie!" She blew her nose into a paper napkin.

Although I actually felt relieved it was nothing worse than a kid lying about homework, I hated seeing Jen so upset. "Jen, I'm so sorry. But isn't that what kids do? See what they can get away with, I mean?"

"Well, yeah, I guess so," she sniffed. "But you see, it's more than that." She paused to collect her thoughts. "This class, this class was like a gift to me. It was like a "thank you, Mom, for giving up your free time to homeschool me." It was my special time. My only time." She looked down at her hands. "Mark never says thank you. Obviously Tim has no respect for me. He sent me off to class so he could play video games! What am I doing wrong?"

I began to understand. Here sat a woman who gave of herself every day, quietly and without reciprocation. Here sat a woman who placed everyone's needs above her own, until she finally wanted to scream out that her own needs mattered. Deep down, we all like to hear words of thanks or praise, to receive some sort of acknowledgement for the sacrifices we make for others. After a while, we have to decide how to handle the silence on the other end.

I thought a lot that day about the nature of giving and what to expect in return. Mark and David gave until their coffers were nearly empty, repeatedly expecting recognition from those who would never give it. Jen also gave of herself repeatedly, and finally thought she had received a thank-you only to have it yanked away.

Some people don't understand when to stop giving. Perhaps they think it is selfish to stop. Is there is a way to give without giving away too much? Giving can be such a pleasure! I much prefer giving to receiving, particularly at holiday time. For years I started months in advance, pouring through catalogs in search of special things my children might like but never ask for, the kinds of things that aren't advertised on TV. Boxes arrived as early as October, and I would open them secretly, hum holiday tunes as I wrapped each gift and tuck everything into hidden basement corners to wait for December.

Christmas morning never lasted long enough. I loved the sound of ripping paper and squeals of surprise, as much as I dreaded the inevitable items that required assembly. As I had done all the purchasing, I had no one to blame but myself. Likewise, I had only myself to blame when I lost the joy of Christmas shopping altogether. All year long, I spoiled my children with clothing, books, treats, outings, and even the occasional CD or video game. Making Christmas more special than any other day began to require not only creativity but extravagance.

It was not my kids' fault that they were no longer excited by ordinary gifts. I had destroyed their enjoyment of receiving, and the pleasure I found in giving, as well. It's not that I was giving to the wrong people or that I expected any thanks; I just gave too much and too often. In order to make Christmas special, I needed to change how I behaved during the other eleven months of the year, not disappoint my children on Christmas morning.

The recession made change not only welcome but necessary. We stopped going out to eat and shopping "just for fun." Our first recession Christmas was the least extravagant and most enjoyed in our recent memory. The kids had not received anything new in such a long time, a book or sweater brought as wide a smile as a Barbie Dream House might have done, two years prior. The extra money we had from our thrift was spent on charity-giving, and I sang louder wrapping clothes for underprivileged teens than I had ever sung wrapping toys for my children.

I wonder if David, and perhaps Mark, as well, had not given to the wrong people after all, but rather had given too much and too often. The employees took their bosses' sacrifice for granted, because they had become accustomed to it. It is hard to appreciate what you've come to expect. We don't wake up every morning saying, "thank you for the ability to breathe," until, perhaps, we come down with pneumonia. Even then, after a few weeks we will once again take breathing for granted. We don't think less of ourselves for not being grateful for such a simple thing; anyone would forget to be grateful for that.

Poor Jen had given too much and too often as well. Tim did not appreciate his mother because her giving, like breathing, had become an expected constant in his life. This may have hurt Jen's feelings but it was her own doing, and good for neither of them. Any change in Tim's feelings or behavior would have to be shaped by Jen's own actions, just as the clay she turned would not become a vase without her patient and concerted intervention. If she succeeded, she would not only enjoy the appreciation she craved, but help her son become a better person as well.

A few weeks later, Jen returned to her pottery class. Every Wednesday Tim now sits in the back of the room waiting, quietly doing math problems, which Jen looks over before leaving the pottery studio. She didn't have to give up her class, or send Tim back to traditional school, in order to get what she wanted. I think Tim is learning as much as Jen, and not just algebra. He is learning that there are consequences to his actions. He is learning to show respect for his mother, following her example as she learns to demand respect for herself.

Green Peppers and Dark Chocolate

Groceries, laundry, housecleaning, errands. All I wanted was a day for me! This was not going to be that day. In retrospect, it could have been. I could have left the dishes in the sink, the laundry in the hamper, the mop in the closet, the shirts at the dry cleaner. I could have put the dog in the car and driven off to the park, or sat on the porch with a book, but I didn't. Any indulgence would have to wait until the house chores were done.

That was typical for me. Also typical: by the time the house chores were done, it was time to go pick up the kids. Opportunity lost, yet again, to take care of myself.

Unfortunately, many moms do the exact same thing. Some work in offices, others stay at home. Some keep their houses meticulously clean, while others believe that neatness is a sign of bad priorities. Some pop frozen dinners into the microwave; others create gourmet meals from scratch. As much as moms can differ, they often share this single trait: putting themselves last on their priority list. Once everyone else is taken care of, they check in. Have I eaten in the last eight hours? Have I exhaled in the last thirty minutes? Am I unraveling?

Off to the grocery store. I usually do not make a list on paper, though I keep a mental list of what we need. Sometimes I end up forgetting the one thing I was most especially there to buy, like milk, bread, or eggs. The essential item requires a return trip the very same day.

My husband has a frequent flyer card; I deserve a frequent shopper card! Not just the "membership" card with occasional discounts, but more like valet parking, red-carpet entry, umbrella escort on rainy days. If a year contains 365 days, and I go to the grocery store 730 times per year, shouldn't I receive some sort of fanfare? Perhaps they can name an aisle after me, reserve a parking space, or put my name on an engraved plaque above the dairy department.

I don't always forget essentials. Often I forget things we don't need, but which I really, really want. For instance, I go to Target with the kids to buy socks, but hope to also pick up a new lipstick or mascara. More often than not, I walk out without it.

Even if the desired item actually makes it to my cart, it tends to fall into the bottom and roll where I can't see it. It never makes the trip to the cashier, and I find it when I unload my bags. Unwanted hide-and-seek. Not fair! I would feel guilty keeping the lipstick and am always in "too much of a hurry" to go back into the store, so I leave it in the cart, hoping that an employee will notice and return it to the display for me. And that shade would have been perfect, too. Oh well.

But never, never, do I arrive home and find extra items in my shopping bag.

On this day, as I unloaded my groceries onto the kitchen counter, two extra items appeared: a green pepper and a small dark chocolate bar. I was flabbergasted. What an unusual pairing of items to show up in my bag! I looked at the pepper; it's dark green, and looks so crisp, healthy, and delicious. The dark chocolate, I knew, was both healthy and a deliciously satisfying indulgence.

Coincidence? I think not. I don't put much stock in coincidences. Things generally happen for a reason, whether or not we can interpret that reason. Sometimes little things are pieces of a bigger puzzle, and we only see the picture years later. Sometimes the message is not for us, but for someone else, in which case, we could bang our heads against a wall for hours and still come up with nothing. I will stubbornly stick with my "reason" theory, even if the mystery cannot be solved. But this? This was a no-brainer.

I knew what I had to do. I had to start taking care of myself better (eating those peppers) and making sure I enjoyed being good to myself (taking a bite of that dark chocolate). I had seen women go to the spa, or play tennis, or take an occasional "girls' night out," and assumed the enjoyment was wrong. If those women were taking care of themselves first, their families must have been suffering in some way from lack of attention.

Maybe I was wrong! Maybe those women need to have fun in order to joyfully slave away later at house chores. Maybe they need to get that new shade of lipstick more than the new sweat socks, so they can feel pretty while they walk the dog around the neighborhood. When you're on an airplane, the flight attendant tells you to put on your own oxygen mask and then help your children. Does that apply to everyday life as well?

As I munched the pepper, I thought about how wonderful it would be to put on my oxygen mask first. No one could do that for me. Inhale. Long, slow exhale. How good it felt! I ate the entire pepper and then the chocolate, enjoying every bite and every breath. Then I left the dishes in the sink and the laundry in the hamper, and went to draw myself a hot bath. For a few miraculous hours, the world revolved around me. I soaked. I did my nails. I read a chapter in my favorite book. I put on a nice outfit and drove enthusiastically to Target, where I chose three new lipstick colors, and treated myself to a cappuccino at the in-store Starbucks.

The kids appreciated how relaxed and happy I was during the drive home from school, but also noticed the mess I'd left when we arrived: dirty dishes, dirty clothes, dirty everything. Looking closer, I also noticed unpaid bills, dinner not started, and the dog in need of going out.

But life felt great! I tied on an apron to cover my good clothes, stuck the kids in front of the TV with a snack, and started chopping vegetables. The kids helped me tidy up while dinner cooked, and I thanked them profusely for all of their hard work. They beamed with pride and went off to start homework. I put a "surprise" in the oven to bake. At six-thirty my husband walked in to find a well-dressed and smiling wife, happy children, a (relatively) neat house, and a kitchen that smelled of warm, healthy dinner and well-deserved brownies.

I remember that day fondly and recreate it whenever I can. Realistically, it can only be accomplished on days without karate, ballet, or art class, and even then, only when I make it a priority. Sometimes weeks will go by 'till I remember to exhale and savor the moment. At least I now understand that my oxygen mask goes on first, and that sometimes I have to put green peppers and dark chocolate into my own shopping cart.

Frustrated Poet

I drove a 1996 black Volvo station wagon. I loved my station wagon. The leather seats were worn through, but that just made them more comfortable. The back was large enough for our two standard poodles, the middle seat wide enough for three children, and the front seats had electric heaters. What we lacked was a working radio. It had a broken cassette player, which we mourned terribly, but the radio breaking meant Mommy had to provide the music. When I ran out of songs I knew, I'd make some up, like this one about my friend's minivan, sung to the tune of "Yellow Submarine" by the Beatles:

We all live in a silver mini van, a silver mini van, a silver mini van.

We drive all day in our silver mini van.

It's hard to keep it clean, but we do the best we can.

Under the seat, there's underwear, Can't imagine how it got there!

There's pizza crust, books overdue, Half-eaten sandwich from 2002...

We all live in a silver mini van, a sticky soda can, an over-flowing dam.

Open the door and who knows just what you'll find?

The piles are so high we may have left someone behind...

My kids always roared with laughter when I sang that one. Of course, there were many more that didn't elicit a single chuckle—some of them because they were sentimental lullabies, and others because, frankly, I'm not always that funny. Now that my kids are older, I limit my singing to songs written by professionals with whom they are unfamiliar. When I try to sing songs they actually know, I run the risk of hearing, "No, Mom. You're doing it ALL WRONG!"

I saw no need to limit myself to songwriting, anyway, when there were so many other arts I could butcher in private. I would try my hand at poetry. Here's what I wrote when we finally got a babysitter and ran off for an evening without the kids:

I found my mom's pearls. I blow-dried my hair.

I put on my favorite black lace underwear.

A night on the town! I felt like a queen:

No dinner to cook and no dishes to clean!

This evening out is a big treat indeed,

And after this week it is just what I need.

My sweet husband whispers, "You look really great."

I order a salad (I'm watching my weight).

He winks and he smiles, gives his belly a pat,

Yells into the speaker, "Yeah, large fries with that!"

OK, that was disastrous! Maybe I'd better stick to what I do best. What is it I do best, again? Oh, right: I am a full-time mom. That must be what I do best. Before I became a full-time mom I worked in an office, and I certainly was not the best. Before that I was a student. Again, not the best. But now I can say certifiably and without a doubt that I am the very best mom in the world. I know because Caitlin told me so. And I quote: "Mom, you're very best mom in the whole wide world!" My daughter is an extremely discerning young lady, so I treasure this compliment and include it right here, forever in print so that when she becomes a teenager and tells me how much I stink, I can prove to her she once thought I "rocked."

I have long since given up being the best mom at any one particular thing. The truth is, as much as I joke about my failings, I know that I am the best mom in the world for my kids. Every mom I know is the best for their kids. In turn, our kids are the best for us, as individuals, and that's how we end up together on this huge planet just teeming with billions of people. Call me crazy if you will, but this is my belief, and it's very reassuring.

I've always enjoyed being a mom. Other moms get tired of zoos, museums, and parks, but not me. I even enjoy amusement parks, though I'm so prone to motion sickness, I get nauseous on a playground swing. Just being around happy kids makes my day. My parents used to think I dragged the kids all over town to avoid having them at home wrecking the place; but the truth is I looked forward to our outings as much as they did. Here is an email I sent my friend Kristen in April of 2008:

Let's see, it took forever to get the kids out of the house. Then the zoo parking lot was overcrowded (they had to close it), so Caitlin screamed a lot and we went to the waterfront park. But the park we usually go to was closed for resurfacing. Caitlin screamed some more. We went to the other waterfront park, where both kids complained for a long time, but we did get some sun and it was a lovely day. Then they whined how hungry they were so we went to the Subway at the Science Center and to the Imax. Then they argued through the museum until it was time to leave, at which point they decided we needed to stay.

I dragged them to the grocery. Caitlin picked one of those cute, unmanageable carts with the little "car" in front, and then refused to sit in it. Andrew kept trying to put her in. She hit him. He yelled at her. They yelled at each other in the odd aisles and exchanged dirty looks in the even aisles.

At checkout, Andrew told Caitlin to get into the "car" so she'd be safe in the parking lot, and she called him a poopy-head.

At that moment, the cashier handed me my receipt and said, "Have a nice night!"

I burst out laughing. Almost couldn't stop. I looked at the cashier. "You've gotta be kidding me!" I told her.

She burst out laughing, too.

Kristen loved that e-mail, and when I read it, I still remember that day as if it were yesterday. I especially remember laughing so hard, I couldn't stand up straight. I hugged my belly and bent in half, my sides silently splitting as I rocked back and forth. Tears streamed from my eyes, my cheeks hurt, and finally the laughs resounded loudly and unabashedly for anyone to hear.

Why waste time writing really bad poetry when life is already so much fun? The kids may be older now, and more mature, and the level of hilarity has decreased significantly, but being a mom is still a full-time job worth having. I clean house (not the best). I cook (again, not the best). I run carpool, do laundry, and accomplish a million other menial tasks each week so that I can be there for the special moments, and not just the side-splitting ones. Andrew may share a new favorite song on his iPod. Caitlin may create a new dance step and perform it in the living room. They may stop bickering long enough for him to help her with homework (which actually happened, and I snapped a photo to prove it). Perhaps it is my enthusiasm for motherhood that makes me the best mom in the world for my children. If this is my most significant qualification, I have nothing to be ashamed of.

Velcro

My son took a while to grow into himself. Now he's so eloquent and wise, funny and polite, kind and generous, but he struggled through his earliest years. He was not exactly hyperactive, but he required a certain amount of input and activity. He was overly sensitive to how others felt about him, yet unable to change behaviors that formed their opinions.

My earliest memory of his eyes was that they did not belong to a baby. They belonged to an adult, thrust back into babyhood and wondering, "What do I do now? Who will take care of me?" Those magnificent hazel eyes looked at me desperately, lovingly, and trustingly. I had no idea how to be a mother, but I knew I could not let those eyes down. I swore to do my best to make his world happy and safe.

Unable to breastfeed, I fed him formula. He spit up a great deal, so our pediatrician eventually switched him to soy. He was still fussy, but we contented ourselves with the notion that we were doing the best we could. He grew at a normal pace and developed ahead of schedule. He spoke early, walked at eleven months, taught himself to read before he turned four. He once told us a bedtime story, and it is still my favorite story in the world: "Once upon a time; Mommy, Daddy, and me; Happily ever after; The end."

Andrew was both adventurous and timid: fearless in the playground and awkward around other children. He had deep circles under his eyes no matter how much he slept, and a surprising expression of concern when placed in a room with other toddlers. Over time, he became boisterous and almost overbearing, like his brain was working too fast. He couldn't temper his enthusiasm or slow his creative connections to the pace of his little playmates.

I used to watch him carefully, waiting to intervene if necessary to adjust his volume or tone down his excitement. Constantly, I walked on pins and needles. The behavior of other children gave me clues as to what was considered normal. Whenever Andrew traveled outside the path of his friends, who were all quieter and calmer than he was, I felt that I had somehow failed him. He was precocious but having trouble fitting in. What good was "smart" if it led to "unhappy?"

Andrew befriended Noah at preschool. Noah was also unusually bright, and the boys got along well. Noah's mother, Shari, and I quickly grew close during frequent play dates. I was relieved finally to be able to relax my guard and enjoy some coffee and conversation with another adult. We could chat for a couple of hours without any complaints from the boys, and then it would be time to pack up and go home. The friendship lasted for years, even after the boys went off to different elementary schools.

I remember the time Noah's friend, John, was also over to play. When John's father arrived to pick him up, John quickly dashed towards the door, got out his shoes, and began to tie his laces. Andrew never dashed to the door unless he was asked not to; he always insisted on "just finishing up." No discipline. He also did not know how to tie laces. Another way I had failed him. As long as there was Velcro, I figured I did not have to fight that battle. We had enough to deal with, without awkward fingers struggling to cross "bunny ears".

When John was safely packed into his father's car, I admitted my failings to Shari. How I was too lax on Andrew and didn't enforce rules well enough. How I had never taught him to tie his shoelaces. How he somehow didn't seem like the other boys.

"Don't be so hard on yourself," she told me. "Kids all have their stuff going on that you don't see. John's parents are going through a divorce, and he's in therapy. He's a troubled kid and acts out a lot at school; Noah is his only friend. Noah isn't perfect, either; you're just not here when he throws his tantrums. Kids are just like grown-ups, they all have issues. Andrew is a great kid, and he'll be fine," she said, reassuringly. "And just for the record, there is nothing wrong with Velcro."

Slam. That was a door slamming open, not shut. My wake-up call. Maybe my boy was just as "normal" as the other kids! Shari wasn't worried about how Noah would turn out, just about how to help him right now. John may appear to be the perfect child, but he was struggling in his own way. And tying shoes was not even worth mentioning.

Once the door opened so did the possibilities, and two wonderful things happened in rapid succession. First, after testing ruled out ADD/ADHD, my mother sent me an article about the Miriam Bender Achievement Center. I called immediately to make an appointment, and Andrew was diagnosed with underdeveloped STNR (Symmetric Tonic Neck Reflex). Simple exercises, performed at home five nights each week, would alleviate his ADD-like symptoms. No medication necessary!

At first the twenty-minute exercises took over an hour to complete. How he hated them! They were difficult and uncomfortable. It was hellish for both of us, but we persevered. Several months in, the exercises took only half an hour. Six months in, we actually enjoyed them. Every six weeks for a year, we had our Five-Hour Fridays: two hours' drive each way to the Center, and a one-hour session for evaluation and new assignments.

The second wonderful thing: Dr. O Dell from the Center told me she suspected Andrew had a severe milk allergy. She noticed the dark circles under his eyes and asked many questions, especially about my pregnancy, his birth, and his early feeding habits. How obvious it seemed once she brought up the subject! I was ashamed of myself for not having figured it out before. We immediately cut out all dairy products, and reduced his gluten intake as well. The circles under his eyes disappeared almost immediately, and he seemed more relaxed and well-rested.

Dr. O Dell, the kindest of women, told me we would never know how much of the change in my son came from the exercises and how much from the alteration of diet. The only thing important to her—and to me—was that Andrew had improved so much. Our first drives to Indiana were miserable, fidgety trips, and the appointments full of "don't touch that!" and "settle down!" By the end of the year, we looked forward to the long drives together, even arriving a little early so we could stop at Burger King for a treat of french fries. My son had become more wonderful than I'd ever imagined he could be.

Without Shari, I would not have had such hope for my child. Without my mother, I never would have learned about the Miriam Bender Achievement Center. Without Dr. O'Dell, I would not have known about STNR or addressed Andrew's food allergies, which contributed to his struggles. These women changed my family's life permanently for the better, and I am eternally grateful.

Once when I shared this story with a friend, she drew attention to the role I had played, persevering with exercises and long Fridays. I vehemently refused her praise. I had only done what any good mother would do. That is, I did the best I could for the child I adore. What else would a mother do?

Motherhood is the ultimate humbling experience. No matter how hard we try, we cannot be perfect mothers; every day offers new opportunities to mess up! Also, as much time, love and effort that we offer, we sometimes lack the expertise required to help our children. In order to do our best for those we love, we accept advice and assistance from family, friends, teachers, and paid professionals. This is not a sign of weakness, but a sign of strength—the strength of putting our children's needs ahead of our own egos. It's a reminder that when we became parents, we took on the responsibility of giving our very best effort, but never promised to do it in a vacuum.

Our children will always be human, not little gods, no matter how much we worship them. No matter how hard we try, our children will sometimes fall or fail, lose a game or a friend. They will learn from those experiences, and hopefully we will, too. We can learn to let them fall once in a while, so that they learn to stand back up on their own. We can learn to give, seek or accept help at appropriate times, to concentrate on the big issues, and to let Velcro take care of the little ones.

Empty Nest

~~~~~~~~~

In *Pride and Prejudice*, the youngest Miss Bennet marries first, and Mrs. Bennet is sorry to see the first of her five daughters leave home:

> *"But my dear Lydia, I don't at all like your going such a way off. Must it be so?"*

> *"Oh, lord! yes; - there is nothing in that. I shall like it of all things."*

In time, they will all leave home. While I am not particularly fond of Mrs. Bennet, Lydia has been her pride and joy. It is a shame that she, of all the girls, should be so heartless towards her dear Mama. I hope I behaved better when I left home for the first time.

I wonder what it feels like to live in an "empty nest." I imagine at first there will be a deep sense of ending and loneliness. I imagine walking through the quiet house, remembering all the good times. I'll go through photo albums. I'll dust their rooms, sit on their beds and wonder what they are doing at that moment, who's laughing at their jokes. I'll notice I'm still buying too many groceries for just two people. When I reach for a jacket, I'll wonder if they're warm where they are.

And then I'll pack a suitcase, and go see the world!

David and I have not spent more than two consecutive days alone together since Andrew was born. That is a long time to wait—thirteen years, as I write this. Ten more years from now, Caitlin will graduate from high school. That's the way we view time: ten more years to enjoy parenthood to its fullest, and ten more years until freedom, or total cosmic meltdown. I'll still be Mom, but it will never be the same again.

My mother never stopped being a caretaker, even after my sister and I went off to college. She cared for both my grand-mothers, until they passed. When her dear cousin Sally died, Mom spent a lot of time caring for Sally's children, and to this day, she provides them with a home-away-from-home. A local senior citizen became my mother's next charge. She acts as her welfare advocate, carts her to and from doctor's appointments, brings her to social events, and in every way makes her feel like a part of the family. Mom always finds someone to take care of. After all, I live 800 miles away. My sister lives 3,000 miles away. What else is a Mom to do?

The next person I heard about was Nadiya. She had come from a local shelter, and needed a place to stay while she enrolled in nursing school. Nadiya has parents of her own, but they live abroad. She traveled halfway across the world to be with a man who became violent once they had married. It seemed natural that Mom would open her door to this woman. Indeed, who would not, after hearing her story? Someone to clothe, cook for, drive around. Someone who needed a Mom, as much as my mom needed to mother someone.

Time passed, and Nadiya stayed. I heard more and more about her. She spoke several languages and had managed a business. Her school records got lost, and now she had to start all over to get a bachelor's degree. "You would love her, Sylvie. She's just like you," Mom said. "She's so smart and gentle. We're on our way out clothes-shopping. It's almost like you were here all over again!" A year passed, and then another year. Nadiya called my parents "mom" and "dad," and she got straight As in school. My parents had their picture taken with her, brought her to the cousins' houses for holidays, and bought her presents on her birthday. We had still never met.

Around the same time, my friend Dara took in a foster child. While Nadiya was in her mid-20s, this boy, Trey, was only fifteen, and greatly in need of stable parenting. Trey was a quiet, handsome boy with huge, deep eyes and an infrequent, heart-melting smile. Dara was in her thirties and single, and had long wanted to share her life somehow. Immediately she called him "son" and dove headfirst into motherhood. Unfamiliar with teenagers, she let him be her guide. He picked out his own clothes, chose his bedding and posters for his new room, and filled the kitchen with frozen pizza, pop-tarts, soda, and spaghetti—the only foods he would eat.

A few short months later, Dara learned she had been misled by the foster agency. They had told her he was passing the tenth grade; not only was he failing, he was reading at a fourth grade level. They had told her he was well-adjusted; he regularly got suspended for fighting. Dara tried to help him, but he refused both counseling and tutoring. She took him to movies and entertained his friends, and was rewarded with slammed doors and strained silence. After almost a year of struggles and tears, she heard the awful words: "You can't tell me what to do anyway! You're not my mother!"

Dara eventually called the agency and asked that they find Trey another home. Her despair was acute. She felt that she had failed Trey, and would never forgive herself for making him leave. "Mothers don't kick children out. The whole point of this was to take someone in, someone who needed the love I have to give. But the agency lied to me. I didn't know what I was taking on. But do any parents know what they're taking on? Kids don't come with guarantees! I guess I wasn't a real parent, after all. Real parents don't give up."

Real parents don't give up. Had she been a real parent? She had loved a child, sacrificed for him, and rearranged her life to make his more comfortable. That sounds a lot like a parent. Perhaps he wasn't really a child. He was practically an adult, his personality formed and his pain deeply engrained. He had spent years closing himself down, shutting out people who would eventually disappoint or abandon him anyway. Can we be parents to adults? If so, what should that picture look like? How can we paint the picture if we aren't really wanted in it?

Dara had thought she was taking in a child; my mother had knowingly taken in an adult. She calls Nadiya "daughter"; Nadiya calls her "mom." What does that make Nadiya to me? Had she entered my mother's world thirty years ago, we would be sisters. We would have shared experiences, helped each other with homework, gone to movies, and traded clothing. Now we are just two people who share a mother, but not even that. She has her own mother. Still, my mother takes her shopping, rejoices in her report cards, and fills the fridge with her favorite foods. She sees my mother every day, and my mother's world revolves around her. I've never even met her, yet she has taken my mother.

I have been replaced.

I now understand how a child feels when their parents bring a new baby home from the hospital, or a new brother or sister from an agency. I'm angry. I don't want to share. I have been replaced. They think she's better than me. She's a better daughter for them, and they will be better parents to her than they were for me. I am still a child, and my parents belong to me. I refuse to share.

How selfish of me. I'm not there to be mothered. Dara endured so much pain in the effort to give love to one who could not accept it, and still endures pain in her "failure." How fortunate for my mother that she found someone to love, someone who would hungrily enjoy all the attention and care she had to offer. I can't refuse to share my mother, because I'm not there to need her, and to make her feel needed. If I were there, maybe Nadiya would not be. And that would be a shame, for both her and my mom.

I'm glad I have ten more years before my nest is empty. I love being a mother, and I understand how my own mother loves it. So yes, I have been replaced, in a way. And it's OK. Really.

The Magic of Hot Chocolate

When I was growing up, the local school bus stop stopped at our driveway. All of the kids from around my street would mill about in front of the house, and then I would know it was time to grab my backpack. Boys and girls, tall and short, outgoing and shy, athletic and clumsy, all coming to my house! For a girl who was never in the "popular crowd," this was an invitation to at least feel included in a motley crew of neighborhood kids headed in the same direction every morning. Once we boarded the bus, I resumed my identity as the quiet girl with a window seat in the back, but for those brief minutes in the driveway, I could play social butterfly. It was like the cup of coffee I enjoy as an adult, an invigorating start to the day.

My favorite mornings without a doubt were the dark, snowy ones. My mother, the consummate hostess, would make us all hot cocoa and invite the kids to come into our mudroom to wait for the bus. There was a lot of stomping of boots, removal of mittens and grateful "thank-yous", followed by sighs and satisfied slurps of warm, chocolaty goodness. I watched the other kids, who had actually already braved the biting cold, and imagined how good it must feel for them to warm their cheeks, fingers, and insides with the steaming cups of cocoa. I imagined their toes wriggling happily inside their snowboots. What a treat my mother provided for them! What a gift to me, because it made my house so desirable a place for other children to be!

I never achieved my mother's knack for socializing with ease. Always a private person, I could enter a party with a huge smile plastered on my face, make a tour of the room with greetings for everyone, and then collapse in a corner, thoroughly exhausted from trying to be someone I'm not. Even now that I'm old enough to be comfortable with who I am, I prefer one-on-one outings to parties and rarely open up to people beyond my tightest circle of friends.

Fast forward about thirty-five years and I am relocating my family across town. The recession caused us to reevaluate the need for our rambling, always-a-project house in an expensive in-town neighborhood. David and I decided, for a host of reasons, that moving to a comparatively small home in the suburbs made a lot of sense.

I had grown up happily in a suburban ranch house. How natural to come full circle! Now that I was a mom with arthritic knees, the attractions of the move overshadowed the loss of ten-foot ceilings and mahogany pocket doors. Remove the financial pressures of the large home, the intricate moldings that required constant dusting, the three flights of stairs I had to maneuver up and down, and replace them with a 1980s ranch in a family-oriented neighborhood, where children ran freely through connected backyards, and people left their doors unlocked like it was Andy Griffith's Mayberry.

This very sensible decision had to be thrust upon children who, of course, had no say in the matter. Packing up became emotionally painful, especially for Caitlin. She was not only the youngest, but also the one who seemed to be losing the most. She cried when people came to take away her wood play set from the backyard; the new house did not have enough even ground. She stammered with anxiety over whether the new owners would paint over the beautiful murals on her bedroom walls. She screamed when I told her that not of all her furniture would fit in her new room; some of it would have to go to the basement. After months of planning and house-hunting, the reality of what the move meant to her hit me like a freight train. She was getting a raw deal. Would she ever forgive me?

In the weeks preceding the move, I told the kids over and over again about the new neighborhood. It had a pool and tennis courts. It was across the parkway from Andrew's best friend, and just a mile away from two of Caitlin's school friends. We could walk to the ice cream store and a pizza place. Caitlin was not impressed. She didn't care about the neighborhood. She'd seen the house; she liked the house. But it wasn't our house. She didn't want to move.

"You will be closer to two of your very best friends!" I offered.

"So? You always drive me there, anyway. How do I know I'll get to see them any more than before?" She is a smart, tough kid.

"Well, you will. And you will be able to make new friends, too. There are lots of kids in the neighborhood, and it's so quiet there, the kids can run between houses without their parents."

She stopped to consider that for a moment. She'd never been allowed to do that before. "But how will we meet anybody to play with?"

"Easy-peasy!" I declared enthusiastically. "I'll throw us our own welcome party! We'll invite lots of people, and I'll rent a bouncy, and it will be great!"

As fate would have it, David would be out of town on moving day. My friend Mindy helped me finish the packing, deal with the movers, and keep the kids distracted. Until the last box made it to the truck, I'd functioned as an automaton. Then, all of a sudden, it hit me. "I'll be outside," Mindy said. "Why don't you and the kids say good-bye to the house."

"Say good-bye?"

"Yes, of course. You have to say good-bye. It's closure. Everyone needs closure."

Exhausted to the core, I finally had to face the reality that we would likely never set foot in this house again. I felt numb. The kids and I wandered from room to room, sharing memories of things that had happened there. Mr. Magic performed in the living room for Caitlin's birthday. We ate Thanksgiving dinner in the dining room. There was the spot where the Christmas tree had stood, then the area in the front hall where we'd played "sled" with styrofoam peanuts and empty shipping boxes. There we'd had breakfast; there we'd watched TV; there we'd put the dog dishes. The guest room, the least used by our family, seemed the safest place to say our final good-bye. Andrew was brave, but Caitlin and I cried.

Luckily we moved in toward the end of summer, a few days before school started. Mindy and I unpacked quickly, and the kids enjoyed rediscovering their belongings and eating out at restaurants. David returned to find pictures hung, the kitchen organized, and books on shelves. He had no idea what we had been through. I had done too good a job making this move look easy. I wanted some pity!

The first few weeks in the new house flew by. The kids went back to the same school and happily rejoined their friends. The morning routine hadn't changed except by becoming easier, without stairs to negotiate during the hunt for shoes or library books. Cleaning house took less than half the time, and the joys of an attached garage were even apparent to Caitlin on those few rainy days. David and I started to feel at home, and we hoped the kids did, too. We had the same furniture (at least, all that would fit), the same artwork, the same clothes, and most importantly the same loving family.

It was a little like the cereal trick. When a box of your child's favorite brand-name cereal is empty, keep it! Buy a generic brand of the same type of cereal, remove the plastic bag with the cereal inside, and place it in the brand-name box. Voila! Most kids can't tell the difference, and you've saved some money. That's what we did, only in reverse. We packed up all our belongings from the fancy "box" and put them in a less expensive box. From the inside, the cereal looked the same. It seemed we'd gotten away with it; we could ignore the box itself. Then one day in September, Caitlin sat down across from me and looked deeply into my eyes. "Well?" she asked. "When is the party?"

"What party, sweetie?" Of course I knew exactly what she was talking about. I had been hoping she'd forget.

"The Welcome Party! The one you said we'd have, to invite over all the kids I get to meet!"

When Mom makes a promise, Mom keeps the promise. So here I was, Introvert Extraordinaire, running off copies of an invitation to stick into strangers' mailboxes.

Come meet us, your new neighbors!

Inflatable Slide for the kids!

Refreshments for all!

I peered into backyards, looking for signs of children: trampolines, bikes, basketball hoops. I slid invitations into the mailboxes. I wondered how many adults we could fit comfortably in our smaller living room, and what sorts of refreshments to prepare. Some RSVPs came in, but not many. I had no idea how many people would actually show up.

The day of the party came during a cold snap in October. The kids would likely be warm enough running around outside, but if they came in, where would I fit them? What would they do? People started to arrive. Before long, we had perhaps fifteen kids in the backyard and twice as many adults milling around the house. No one seemed to be eating anything, and I felt like I had put out way too much of all the wrong food. I tried to be a good hostess, put on my best party-smile and introduced myself. Many faces were already familiar, and we are blessed with extremely wonderful neighbors. But this party was not really for me. As I said, I am not a party person. This was for my children, and especially for Caitlin.

I made several trips out the back door to check on the kids. The bouncy slide that arrived in the morning took up half the driveway and reached higher than the gutters on the garage. The kids loved it! Parents chatted comfortably on our small patio, wearing light jackets and friendly smiles, and I offered them refreshments. After an hour or so, the children were tired, ruddy-cheeked, and wanting to come inside for warmth. Luckily I had learned a lesson from my mother: hot chocolate makes magic.

"Come on in, kids!" I called out. "Hot chocolate and cookies are ready!"

"Hot chocolate? Yeah! All right!" came the excited squeals.

The kids pushed their way into the kitchen. Unfamiliar faces that would soon become regulars in our lives. New friends. I grabbed a ladle and headed for the steaming cocoa that had been warming on the stove. Cup after cup made its way to the table, followed by gentle plops of marshmallows and the happy quiet slurping into satisfied tummies.

"Your mom makes the best hot chocolate ever!" said one boy.

"May I have some more?" a girl asked, holding up her mug.

"Pass the cookies!" cried another boy.

One look at Caitlin's shining face made the entire party worthwhile. Just like my mother before me, I had offered hot chocolate to a neighborhood full of boys and girls, tall and short, outgoing and shy, athletic and clumsy. I imagined how good it must feel for them to warm their cheeks, fingers, and insides with the steaming cups of cocoa. Caitlin got to be the social butterfly and enjoy the company of children who thought her house was a great place to be. The move had felt cold and harsh, like winter in the middle of summer. Now, when the world around us had started to cool off for real, we had the joy of new friends to warm us.

Other People's Children

"It's shocking the way children behave," muttered one woman to another. They sat comfortably in a booth at McDonald's, sipping McCoffees and eating McMuffins, wiping the corners of their mouths with McNapkins. Down their long, pointy noses they viewed a toddler dipping pancake pieces into syrup and then using them to decorate the top of his head. (Quite artistically, I might add.)

"Did she do that herself?" a woman asked a young mother, looking at the girl sitting in her grocery cart. The girl wore one long pigtail on the right side. On the left was a very short pigtail, because she'd cut the rest off with Mommy's sewing scissors. "No!" replied the mother emphatically. "It's the newest look. You have to pay extra for that, and only the most exclusive salons will do it for you."

Yes, it is amazing and sometimes shocking what children will do, and even more amazing that childless people often miss the humor in it! New mothers tend to be more high-strung, but even they mellow out eventually. It took me a while to laugh at the sight and sound of my three-year-old spread-eagle in the middle of Target with her hands gripped tight to a toy

I refused to buy, face red with screaming, feet kicking wildly. The trick is not to laugh in front of the kid. It's not as easy as you'd think. Here, let me explain how it's done.

First, turn off your ears. Chocolate calories don't count on Christmas, and screams you don't hear can't raise your blood pressure. Next, pretend no one else is in the store. They'll only offer pity, advice, or judgment, and you've got enough to deal with. Finally, be grateful for all of the heavy groceries you've been lifting, because your biceps make Hercules look like Paris Hilton. Pry the toy away, scoop your precious angel off the floor, and toss her over your shoulder. (If she's too big, a basket-carry will do, but make sure the arms and legs are facing away.) Stick her in the car, buckle her into the safety seat, and drive around town. For an hour, if you have an hour to spare.

When you get home, gently lift her sleeping body out of the car and tuck her into bed. Admire the way her hair spills around her face, the flush of her chubby cheeks, and the gentle movements of her fingers as she clutches her blanket. Be grateful that you've been blessed with such a magnificent creature, and know in your heart that she won't be three forever. Quietly close the door and tiptoe over to the liquor cabinet. Pour yourself a double of something on the rocks, and pray she doesn't wake up 'til your glass is empty.

The younger the child, the cuter the transgressions. Even endless questions are tolerated longer when issued from a tiny mouth: "Why is my peanut butter sticky? If you put my bread in the blender, would it get sticky too? Could you bake my peanut butter and make it hard, and then spread blender-bread on top? Would that taste any different from the other way around? Why don't people sell blender-bread, 'cuz then you could just eat your sandwich with a spoon and not have to wash your hands first? Did you wash your hands before you made my sandwich? 'Cuz I didn't wash mine before I ate it!"

As children grow older we expect more out of them, and it's extremely satisfying to watch them mature. I once had charge of a ten-year-old boy. I had explained to him, and to his mother, that he could spend the afternoon at our house playing video games, but we'd have to stop at the mall first. In just two days, my son Andrew had to attend an occasion that required slacks and jacket, and he'd outgrown everything he owned. "No problem!" his friend convinced me. "I'm stuck shopping with my family all the time. I'm used to it. I'll be quiet as a mouse."

The well-behaved boys rode quietly to the mall and followed behind me through the men's department. (Andrew is very tall.) I grabbed blazers in two different sizes and led Andrew towards a large mirror so he could try them on. "Are you going to let him keep his T-shirt on? Because blazers always look different when you have a dress shirt on," his friend offered.

"That's true," I replied. "Thank you for the thought, but I really just want to see if they fit. That will make the shopping go quicker so you boys will have more time to play." He nodded in agreement. Andrew slipped on the first blazer. "Looks good, Andrew, but you've got no room to grow. Let's try this other one."

"You know," the friend interrupted, "if you want the shopping to go quicker, let's just grab three sizes of jackets and pants, and buy them. You can return the extras later. Then we're out in five minutes. That's what my mom does."

"I appreciate that," I answered, beginning to feel annoyed, "but I don't have time to go back and forth to the mall. It'll only take a few minutes, I promise." The second jacket fit perfectly. "See!" I exclaimed happily. "Let's just find pants and we're good to go."

As we turned to leave the jackets area, the Hoover dam burst. My fight-or-flight response kicked in as I sensed the rapid torrents approaching, but decorum forced me to stand and face the flood head-on. Terrified, I clenched my fists and hoped I would be strong enough to hold my ground. "Actually, we've already been here for nine minutes. If you count the time it took to get from the car into the mall, and then from the mall entrance into the store, that adds another four minutes. You got a really good parking space! My mom never gets such a good parking space. Anyway, add the time it took to get from my house to the mall, wow, that's a total of like, twenty-three minutes! That's enough for us to get through three and a half levels of a two-person shooter-game. It makes more sense for you to come back tonight, after your husband gets home, and just bring home a few pairs of pants in different sizes. That's what my mom would do."

For a split second I secretly indulged myself in a vision of this boy gagged and duct-taped into a wheelchair so we could get our shopping done. I would have traded him in for three screaming toddlers, maybe even four, because they're so cute and because their tantrums don't mean anything. Much less annoying than a kid who's starting to look like a little adult, and who should know better than to tell someone else's mother how to shop!

If it were my own kid, I wouldn't put up with this. But of course, my kid would never tell me what to do. Andrew might express boredom or dislike of trying things on, but he always does so respectfully and in ten words or less. I didn't want to shop for pants, but I had to. I didn't want to have this kid with me, but here we were. And I couldn't discipline him because he was someone else's kid.

Sometimes other people's children are polite but find other ways to leave their mark on your day. One very sweet friend of my daughter's, for example, responsibly covered our kitchen table with newspaper before embarking on a project using glow-in-the-dark inks. She said "please" and "thank you," and piled all the newspapers in the recycle bin when they were finished. I was so impressed! When her mother came to fetch her, she stopped playing and came to the door without complaints, and told me what a nice time she had. Shortly after she left, I found her wet artwork face-down on the dining room table. I managed to peel it off, but the special inks had permanently stained her name, mirror-image, into the fine wood finish. That playdate cost me four hundred dollars, plus shipping to and from the refinishers.

Thus we see that the level of humor we find in children's antics depends on several factors, including (but not limited to) our years of mothering experience, whether or not the child belongs to us, and the expense involved. New mothers "tut tut" at other children's toy store tantrums but blush in horrified mortification when their own children pitch a fit. Experienced mothers handle their own children with aplomb but sometimes crumble when faced with someone else's troublesome tyke. As for expense, let's just say I never found the humor in that table incident.

One truly great thing about other people's children is that they make us appreciate our own. Ill-behaved children remind us to teach our own kids manners, and to be grateful when they practice them. Naughty children remind us to teach our own kids morals, and to be sure we set an example for them to follow. We should try to remember that other people's children deserve as much patience and understanding as our own, and that our own little angels are "other's people's children" to someone else.

GRANDMOTHERS

GRANDMOTHERS

While some rare people still believe that "mother knows best," very few believe that our grandparents' wisdom can't be outdone by a quick Google search, Web MD inquiry, or YouTube tutorial. Grandparents likely need help setting up their computers, sending e-mail attachments, or even using their cell phones. Whatever old-fashioned tidbits they have to offer do not appeal to the new generation. The world is different now. Values are different, time moves more quickly, and young people know far more far earlier than ever before. Older people just don't get it.

I am one of the very few out there who prefer the speed of life that my grandparents experienced. The simplicity of their existence does not seem lacking to me at all. My Grandma Sadie, born in 1910, once told me that she had seen enough change in her lifetime. Radio, "talkies," telephones, televisions, space travel, computers—it was all overwhelming to her. She had been trained as a bookkeeper, and still kept meticulous household records in oversized ledgers yellow with age. She wrote actual, handwritten letters, and knitted us lap blankets in our school colors. David and I gave her our old microwave, and she would watch in fascination as her bowl of soup turned around and around, ready to eat in less than a minute. A miracle! That was enough technology for her.

For me, she provided the voice of wisdom that the rest of the outside world failed to provide. Life outside whizzes by too fast for deep reflection. Sound bites, blogs, and articles offer quick-fixes on everything from careers to relationships to which cleanser is best for such-and-such flooring. But somehow they always leave me unsatisfied. I'm not in that much of a hurry. It was always worth the wait, to get an answer meant just for me.

Grandma's old stories somehow helped me through my new struggles. No self-indulgent "woe is me" could withstand the perspective created by eighty years of life experience, and the profound understanding, after all that time, of what really matters. Nothing comforted me better than a warm, marshmallow hug from someone who loved me simply because I had been born.

I missed Grandma Sadie when I went away to college. Then after David and I married, we spent three glorious years living in Manhattan, near my grandmother. Every Tuesday, my boss would let me leave early so I could trek across town for dinner with Grandma. Some weekends we would watch TV in her apartment, or even go to a movie. One Saturday after a matinee, she told me: "You should go out with your new work friends, Sylvie! You don't have to spend all of your time with an old lady. I'll be fine."

"But Grandma," I choked. "You're my best friend! Isn't it OK for me to go out on the weekend with my best friend?"

Grandma inhaled deeply. I knew she was happy. "Yes, dear. It's OK."

My grandmothers became best friends before my parents got married. "Even if the kids don't get married, let's be friends forever!" they had promised. Two friends could never be closer, or more different. My mother's mother, Rose, was an exuberant blonde who loved to be the center of attention. She had been a trailblazing career woman for her time, loved to have her hair and nails done, always the life of the party. Sadie, an understated brunette, kept within a small circle of close friends, stayed close to home and never wore an ounce of makeup.

As naturally as Sadie took to grandmotherhood, Rose fought it, or at least the nomenclature. The love came easily, but accepting senior status…not so much.

In many ways, Rose was younger than I've ever been, and continued to be young until the day she died. She loved friends and family, doing the crossword puzzles (in ink, not pencil), teasing and joking, and above all, looking pretty and looking at pretty things. As time passed and her glasses got thicker, almost everything looked pretty to her. Let other people get Lasik surgery; I'm hoping for those thick, rose-colored bottle glasses when I become a senior.

To date, I have spent almost half of my life in formal education. School, any school, was always my favorite place. Libraries, lecture halls, workshops, and study groups provided me with thrills of discovery, challenge, accomplishment, and belonging. Yet the greatest teachers I ever had never went to college themselves. Though I studied religion, science, and philosophy at school, my grandmothers' lessons better explained the world and our parts in it. Though I studied law, sociology, and management at school, my grandmothers provided me better insight into justice, humanity, and the intricacies of interpersonal politics.

My formal diplomas are somewhere in the basement, in a dust-covered box, and have long lost significance. My informal diplomas, from my grandmothers, are part of every day I live. To my wonderful teachers, I say, "Thank you. You are not forgotten."

Spoons and Pages

G randma Sadie had a collection of tiny spoons. Souvenirs of days long past, they lay undisturbed in their clear plastic cases, tucked into a drawer by an elderly woman who rarely even ventured from her apartment. I hear in my head someone else's voice saying, "Junk! Just waiting for someone to come and throw them away." Luckily, I ignore some of the voices in my head.

Imagine yourself a stranger in this apartment. You enter and immediately notice a small, step-in kitchen on your right. There is nothing noteworthy to be found. The appliances are outdated, the tile desperately needs replacing, and the cabinets are hanging on for dear life. You pull open one rickety drawer with a slightly rusted handle, and there you find the spoons. But wait! Don't close the drawer. Look closely, and you may be surprised. Some of them traveled quite a long way to reach that drawer: Las Vegas, Hawaii, and Alaska. Singapore, Tokyo, and Hong Kong.

Walk next into the living room, where you notice the figure of a dancing girl from India, who wobbles gracefully when you set her in motion. A screen in the corner may be an authentic

Japanese landscape, and an illustrated book of Persian poetry on the shelf gleams with gold lettering. The scissors in the red case by the sewing kit have handles shaped like bird's wings, and the thimbles inside the kit bear the names of various cities in Europe. Who lives here? Tucked into the frame of a mirror you find a black-and-white photograph of a younger Sadie, twisted into a yoga pose you wouldn't even attempt with a pipe cleaner.

How similar Grandma was to that spoon from Singapore! Who would ever have known she had traveled such distances and had so many stories to tell? Tucked away neatly in her own little case, just like the spoons inside her drawer: inside the studio apartment, in a building of literally hundreds of apartments, on a block you'd pass without stopping, in a city of millions and millions of people. She and her spoons were virtually invisible. Most of my life, even I didn't even know that Grandma had traveled the world. To me, her world was 800 square feet of paint-thick walls and parquet floors that creaked under our feet.

Gran's studio fit snugly into a corner on the eighth floor of a building spanning an entire block. The doorman's face was the only friendly sight between the sidewalk and Gran's own door. Our footsteps echoed in the cavernous, marble foyer, making me feel like we were somehow trespassing. We passed a seating area that no one ever sat in. We gathered Gran's mail from a huge, empty mailroom with endless rows of locked mailboxes. We waited a long time for the elevator, and after silently counting the "dings," we exited for the long trek down an empty, faded hallway with bare stubbly walls and a worn carpet. I looked and listened for any sign of life behind the dozens of mysterious doors, impatient to reach Gran's place and enter a world I loved.

"Hello, house!" she would call out, as she stepped inside and dropped her keys on the side table. "Hello, house!" I would mimic enthusiastically as I headed for the usual tour. First I opened the music box on the side table to hear the sweet song play while I glanced at familiar photos on the bureau. Then I hurried to set aquiver the dancing girl figurine and to check the collection of elephants on the shelves for any new additions. Inside the kitchen were drawers full of wonderful things: a potato masher, an apple-corer, the spoon collection, chopsticks, and all sorts of unusual bowls. Her living room held the largest sectional sofa I'd ever seen, and she'd let me take off all of the pillows to make castles and secret clubhouses. The extra leaf of her dining room table became a slide. I could imagine no place more wonderful than Gran's.

Many happy years went by. I loved being the center of her attention, as all children do. She heard about my lost teeth, the time I won the spelling bee, fights with my little sister, my first boyfriend. Eventually I graduated from high school, and of course she came for the ceremony. The gift she brought appeared like magic: a documentation of my life. Four albums full, beginning with my birth announcement and continuing with photos, letters from camp, drawings, newspaper clippings, concert programs, and copies of report cards. It was proof, somehow, that I had once been tiny and then had grown, and that I had been adored every step of the way.

Armed with this proof of how wonderful I was, I went off to college. This was my time for adventure, time to gather some spoons of my own and see the world. I got off to a glamorous start, hooking up with the Greek god on the next hall over during freshman orientation. Alexis was from Athens, and half-Swedish, a six-feet-three-inch tall hunk of Greco-Swede. He seemed exotic and fascinating (everything I was not but wanted so much to be). I couldn't wait to tell Gran all about him.

I left out some things. His shoes, for instance, were the size of Thanksgiving turkeys, and unfortunately smelled like he stored raw turkeys in them. He used to air them by suspending them between the screen and glass of his window for hours at a time, perhaps making an artistic statement about the connection between size and stench. I was allergic to his Greek laundry detergent and broke out in a rash every time I got close to him. Poor boy rewashed every stitch of his clothing in Tide just for me. Can you imagine? For me! Gran would love to hear that part.

I soon had even more exciting news for Gran: I became a cheerleader. Before you get the wrong idea about me, please understand that being a cheerleader was as unfavorable a claim at my college as it was esteemed in high school. No, I had not become "cool." We did have a football team, but the most popular sport at school was Ultimate Frisbee. None of us so-called cheerleaders could do a split, very few could manage a decent cartwheel, and there were barely enough girls to put together a good half-time show. But we had adorable outfits and pom-poms to shake, and my parents drove in to see the homecoming game.

Unfortunately the gods and I were not meant to be (Greek or otherwise). A few weeks into college my new relationship ended, and sometime during basketball season, the cheerleading squad disbanded. I had lost my claim to being anything other than single, studious, nondrinking, early-to-bed-early-to-rise: in short, a bore. I hung out in the library or the student center, was home by midnight even on Saturdays. How could I entertain Gran on the phone with stories of a spinster-in-the-making? Would a woman who never got to finish high school be interested in hearing about my courses in existentialism? I should have wonderful stories to tell her, something to make it worth the ring of the phone. Something for another page in the albums.

Three and a half years later, I graduated. Now I had another opportunity to make something new of myself, something better and different, and I grabbed it. A large company hired me to work in an area office just outside a major city. I figured it would be a foot in the door and the start to a real career. But instead of learning the ropes, I wanted to hang myself with one. Entry-level turned out to be a code word for "boring." Everyone there was older than I was; I had no friends and nothing to do.

I felt lost and without ballast or compass. I couldn't call Gran. Poor Gran, sitting all alone in that dingy apartment waiting for me to tell her something fabulous and, well, page-worthy! Out of desperation, I joined a singles' group. For months I smiled awkwardly at anything that breathed, and then finally a guy named Howard asked me out. There were no fireworks here, and I truly doubted my future husband could possibly be named "Howard," but this would be a harmless night out and a movie I didn't have to sit through alone.

We met at an Italian restaurant around the corner from the movie theatre. Howard dressed up for our date and actually looked great, even with his receding hairline and dorky glasses. Gran would approve. The lasagna was awesome, though I wished I could douse the bland conversation in parmesan. During dinner, Howard rushed over to buy our movie tickets. The bill arrived while he was gone, and I didn't know what to do, so I paid it. After the movie, Howard insisted on pulling over and buying two pints of Ben & Jerry's to bring back to my apartment. I figured it was his way of apologizing for my having to buy dinner.

Howard opened the car door for me and walked me to my building. He smiled. I smiled back. He handed me the bag with the two pints of ice cream. "Thanks!" he said. "I had a very nice time. Enjoy the ice cream!" With that, he turned on his heel and sort of sprinted back to his car. I stood on the stoop and watched him drive away. I had been paid off in ice cream. I felt like an ice cream slut. There hadn't even been a kiss, so how could I feel so...cheap?

I had nothing to tell Grandma, so I didn't call her at all. I couldn't bear to imagine her disappointment. "Hi, Gran! How are you? Me, oh, well, this guy bought me take-out ice cream and burned my phone number. My job? Well, yeah, it sucks!" What a thrill of a granddaughter I was turning out to be.

At what point did that confident little girl, the center of her grandmother's universe, become ashamed to make a phone call? Why did I think I had to live life for her, as if she'd never had one of her own? I understand now that Gran would have loved to hear from me as much if I had been head cheerleader or head geek. She would have distracted me with family stories while I sat eating all of that Chunky Monkey ice cream, told me my first job was one of many and not to judge myself by it. She wouldn't have loved me any less because I had hit a bump in the road. I still had time to travel, to collect my spoons, and find my way in life. After all, I hadn't loved her for her accomplishments. I loved her because she was my Grandma, she loved me because I was her granddaughter, and it really was that simple.

Now that she is gone, I understand the depth of her love and the meaning of those albums she put together for me. To her, I was always that same little girl writing from camp, playing in the violin recital, happy with my books, and she loved me just the way I was. I should dust off those albums she made for me and open each one. Not out of vanity, but to receive the hugs and acceptance tucked under the plastic of every page.

Cars and Ferkle Elefunks

Contrary to popular belief, the luckiest people in the whole wide world are not the richest. Or the most famous. Or the most celebrated. I am convinced that the "luckiest" people are those who are content with their lot in life, whatever that lot might be, and regardless of suffering, regrets, mistakes, or any other difficulties life may have shown them. My Grandmother Sadie was one of those lucky people. And I am lucky to have known her.

Grandma Sadie had her own style. She wore lots of purple ('ferkle', she called it), long, jangly necklaces, and no makup, ever. Grandma named her cars after royalty and thanked them, when she reached her destination, for conveying her there safely. She sang to traffic lights to make them turn green: "Red light, red light, please turn green. You are the slowest light the world has ever seen!" She would time her song carefully, secretly watching the light on the other side turning yellow, and then poof! Just at the right moment, the light would change. "Thank you very much!" she would sing, and my little sister and I were amazed. Surely Grandma had magic powers! Decades later, I sang the Red Light song to my son in front of my mom. She elbowed my dad and said, "See! Sadie's not dead! She's sitting here in the car with us."

I like to think she's in the car with us, or at least sitting up there in heaven with my other grandmother, Rose, on a comfortable cloud with a front-row view of my life. "Look!" she calls to Rose. "Sylvie is running late for morning carpool again. Quick, get the popcorn! Yes, she's trying to put on mascara before getting the kids their cereal. Ooh, it's gonna be even closer than yesterday. Now she's blaming Caitlin for not putting her shoes on! I'll bet you five notches on the halo she'll lose her keys on the way out the door!"

Like Sadie, I named my car. Her cars had been Princess, Queenie, and Duchess. I drove a dented Volvo station wagon with 150 thousand miles on it, so I named her Bessie. Good ol' Bessie. That historic September 11, 2001, I packed Bessie with my toddler and everything I could squeeze into the trunk, and drove from Atlanta to Louisville without stopping. And Bessie, that great, creaking, clunking beast made it the whole way without once complaining. The world had its eyes on New York, but I had mine only on the road as I headed desperately to be in my husband's arms while we pondered the world situation. I'm glad Bessie had a name; she earned one. "Thank you, Bessie. Thank you for carrying us here safely," I whispered.

I learned a lot from Gran—not just about cars, but about having fun and being an individual. She knew lots of silly poems and said very silly things. When she was full, she wanted air pudding with wind sauce for dessert. Her favorite color was ferkle (purple), and she collected elefunks (elephants). She kept her supply of cigarettes and lighters beneath her framed Smoke-Enders graduation certificate. She watched numerous game shows every night, calling out the answers as if they could hear her, and she kept meticulous records of her investments, savings, and spending on very official-looking bookkeeper paper that no one ever looked at.

Most people didn't know these things about her. That is how a single person can actually be many different people and live different lives all at once. We all see her from our own perspective, colored by our personal experiences and the stories we may have heard. The more private a person is, the more varied the versions of their life become. The women who met her at Mah-Jong as Sarah probably never knew she became a bat-mitzvah at age sixty-three. The other adults in her bat-mitzvah class probably never knew she had studied yoga and traveled to India.

When I was in my teens and twenties, I wasted a lot of time trying to reinvent myself. I believed I could create different versions of myself in this very same way; new people would see only the "me" that I presented. There was Sylvia in the orchestra, Sylvia the cheerleader, Sylvia the partier. Of course the old version of me eventually snuck back into view every time.

That was the flaw in my plan: none of the other versions of me were truthful. Grandma never tried to remake herself the way I did; instead, the real Sadie was a combination of all of the Sadies or Sarahs you might meet. There was just so much to her, no one person held the complete picture except, perhaps, Sadie herself.

The day of Grandma's funeral, one of her friends from synagogue came to me and sobbed on my shoulder. "What a wonderful woman," she said. "We'll all miss her. I hear you are giving the eulogy. I'm sure you'll mention her marvelous elephant collection. That's how I will remember her."

Elephants. Elefunks, as Grandma would have said. She will be remembered for her elefunks? They were not in my eulogy; I had too many other things to say about Grandma, and none of them had to do with trinkets. Grandma had studied Buddhism, and lived a serene and simple life. She collected elephants not because she wanted them, but because people kept giving them to her.

It amused me to think that her menagerie of about fifty elephant figurines had been added to over decades by people who likely had no idea what they symbolize. On various occasions, they chose to give Grandma an elephant "because she collects them," and in this way the collection came into being. Even I had given Grandma elephants, without thinking much about it. Mindless giving.

I'm not surprised, though, that she ended up with them; elephants fit Grandma perfectly. Eastern teachings idolize the elephant, which symbolizes wisdom, patience, power, and dignity. Elephants have proven themselves to be incredibly intelligent, caring, and devoted creatures. Indeed, Grandma was an elephant.

Years later I began a practice of mindful giving. I gave friends purple elephants, or I should say, ferkle elefunks, to commemorate Grandma's birthday because they represent so much of her personality. She was lots of fun, yes, but also noble, wise, and nurturing. She moved deliberately, slowly, and gracefully through her long, full life.

Purple elephants represent almost everything to which I aspire, and everything that Grandma seemed to have achieved. Sadie played many roles in her lifetime: daughter, sister, wife, mother, mother-in-law, grandmother, friend, traveler, companion, book-keeper, Jew, Buddhist. In each role, she remained true to her elephant soul, and I will miss her for that.

Kumquats

When I was eight-years-old, Grandma took me to California in a Boeing 747. I have never been on one since, and know few people who have ever had the opportunity to fly on the "Queen of the Skies," as it was sometimes called. Because it was my very first flight, I probably assumed all airplanes were that large. It was actually twice the size of the usual transcontinental plane, and had a second-story lounge for first-class passengers. Even if I had known how special the plane was, nothing could overshadow the fact that I was on vacation without my parents, heading three thousand miles west.

I kept a journal of the trip, so I remember almost everything. Our flight out was delayed by six hours. While we sat on the runway, I ate eleven bags of potato chips—not the greasy kind, but the almost surreal, light chips that may or may not have any real potato in them. I was hungry, and they were really good. "Are you sure those aren't making you sick?" Grandma kept asking. But there was nothing else to eat! I was the only child on the flight, and everyone was really nice to me. The flight attendant gave me a brand new deck of cards, and the man sitting next to us, Jim, chatted with Gran about our plans for vacation. After a while, the captain himself came over to invite us up to the lounge. We climbed a winding staircase up to a fancy room with comfortable chairs attached to the floor, and a great view of the airport through the large windows. I drank a Sprite with ice in a real glass—not plastic. I remember saying "wow" a lot. If we'd never made it to California, I doubt I would have been disappointed.

Finally the plane took off. I loved watching the landscape grow distant until it disappeared below the clouds. It was magical! I had butterflies the whole time, wondering what California would be like. Grandma's sister, Aunt Charlotte, and her husband, Uncle Moe, met us at the airport. Aunt Charlotte was tiny, even shorter than Grandma, and hardly taller than me. Her eyes twinkled when she smiled, and I knew right away I would like her. Uncle Moe was short, too, but he was stocky and looked quite gruff. Grandma gave him a big hug and a kiss, so he couldn't be all that bad, and I decided I would try to like him, too. He even bought us cold drinks before we left the airport. I sat quietly with my hands in my lap and watched the grown-ups interact. It suddenly dawned on me how far away I'd travelled from home, and I wondered whether I was really old enough for so much adventure.

As we drove to Aunt Charlotte's house, she and Grandma talked without stopping. They certainly seemed to enjoy each other's company, and they hadn't seen each other in years. I couldn't imagine living on the opposite side of the country from my sister. I tried to process the fact that they were family—just like my sister and me—but it seemed impossible that this stranger had grown up with Grandma. She seemed to know things about her that I never would! I felt jealous and confused. This old woman with gray hair and wrinkles reminisced about climbing trees with my grandmother. My grandmother doesn't climb trees. She watches game shows on TV and plays canasta. Am I in the right car?

The world grew before my eyes. The air tasted different in California, and even the sun didn't look the same. Charlotte and Moe owned a fruit ranch in Palm Springs that amazed me, stretching far as the eye could see. Uncle Moe handed me a large cloth sack, showed me how to pick the oranges, and told me I could explore on my own— and pick as many oranges I wanted! I'd pick an orange, put it in the bag, and eat two oranges. Juice ran down my chin and arms, and I'd never tasted anything so fresh and wonderful in my life. The sky was tremendous and warm and blue, the trees so magically green, and the sweet, sweet oranges made me forget how far away I was from home. While we were at the ranch, the world shrank again 'til I was the only one in it. The sky, the trees, the oranges: they were all for me.

Grandma encouraged me to try lots of new things while we were on vacation. She took me to a farmer's market, where she first bought me a Chinese pastry shaped like a butterfly. It didn't taste as good as it looked, and it was very sticky. I saw some tiny oranges and wanted to try those, too. Grandma bought a small bag to satisfy my curiosity. "If you like them, I'll buy you some more, but try them first. These aren't oranges, they're kumquats," she told me. "Eat slowly, you can eat the skin. Try that and then the rest. Be ready for a surprise." I did as she directed, peeling off a bit of the skin with my teeth and chewing. It was good! Then I bit into the heart of the fruit and got a shock of sour. I remember the incredible contrast of sweet and sour, and the amazement of finding something that looked familiar but was actually quite different.

We stayed with Charlotte and Moe for a week at their house in Beverly Hills. It was a small house but it had a nice pool, and I loved to swim. Aunt Charlotte and Grandma would sit by the pool sipping iced tea, and I would cry out, "Watch this! Watch me!" as I dove and flipped and raced through the water. They also let me go on walks around the neighborhood all by myself, and I felt very grown up. Grandma made sure I had my watch with me, and told me I had to be back in an hour. I carefully noted every turn so that I could backtrack without getting lost. After twenty minutes I'd always turn around, not wanting to be late and never knowing how much more time it took to walk back up the hills I'd run down. I enjoyed the independence, the glow of the sun, and the hugeness of the sky. I also enjoyed the escape, not just from older people in general, but specifically from Uncle Moe.

Moe could have been cute, like an older Mickey Rooney, but he was grumpy—more like a short, pudgy version of Scrooge. And he yelled. I was afraid of Uncle Moe. When he was around, I tried to stay quiet and out of his way; after all, I was only eight and he was not used to having a kid around. I peered around corners and noticed how kindly he treated Aunt Charlotte. He would sneak up from behind and give her a hug or a quick peck on the cheek. He would refill her glass of iced tea, and fetch her purse for her when it was time to go to the store. It was very confusing to me, noticing how lovingly he treated Aunt Charlotte, and reconciling that with the man who yelled at a little girl. I behaved the very best I knew how, but still he got angry with me. Why did he yell, and why didn't Grandma stop him from yelling?

One morning in the garden, Grandma sat me down for a talk. "We're going to have a grown-up talk, Sylvie," she said, "because you have proven you're old enough and mature enough to understand grown-up things." I sat quietly and paid very close attention; I had never been talked to like a grown-up before. This must be important, and that scared me a little. "You've seen Uncle Moe take those pills that he carries around?" I nodded. "Those are for his heart. It's not working properly, you see, and sometimes it even hurts him. Uncle Moe is afraid, sweetie. He's afraid that if his heart stops working and he gets really sick, he won't be able to take care of Aunt Charlotte and the other people who count on him. Sometimes when he is scared, or when the pains come, he yells. He isn't angry at you, honey; he's angry at his heart. But he can't yell at his heart. He needs to yell out loud. He doesn't mean to scare you. Do you understand?"

"Yes, Grandma, I do. Thanks for explaining it. I really do understand." For the rest of our visit in California, I felt sorry for Uncle Moe and his heart, and didn't mind as much when he yelled at me. I understood, for the first time, that adults and children weren't always that different, and that in this one instance, I could be the adult while Uncle Moe was the child. Sometimes when I'd lost a kickball game at school, or messed up on a spelling test, I'd come home and yell at my little sister even though she hadn't done anything to deserve it. I just needed to yell, and so did Uncle Moe. I could be brave and deal with it 'til it was time to go back home, because I knew something most people never would: Uncle Moe was like an inside-out kumquat—the sour on the outside, and the sweet hidden within.

Special Food, Special Clothes

G randma Sadie had a tiny kitchen and didn't cook much, but she enjoyed preparing food. She knew just what we liked, too: her "famous" crustless peanut butter and mint jelly sandwiches cut into triangles, and the messiest of crunchy tacos overflowing with cheese and shredded lettuce. She always set the table carefully, with woven place mats and cloth napkins. "But Gran," I'd protest, "but Gran, it looks so fancy. It's just for you and me!" And she'd reply, "So, who is more important than us?"

Many of my food-related memories of Grandma came from my parents' house in the suburbs. Grandma planted a tomato garden in our side yard. They smelled funny in the garden, but tasted so good. We put them in salads, and sliced them for sandwiches. She'd drive up from the city on a Sunday morning, unpack her trowel and gardening gloves, and get to work. She must have been thrilled when my parents moved out of the city and got a house with a yard. There she saw so much life take root: her tomato garden and her grandchildren. At the end of the day, she'd pack up and drive back to her little square of space in the concrete block in the concrete city, to wait for the next weekend.

Holiday celebrations took place in the suburbs as well. Gran would sing contentedly while she assembled pyramids of sandwiches for my parents' annual New Year's Day party: egg salad, tuna salad, and olive-and-cream-cheese sandwiches, all crustless and cut into triangles. Mom would always go behind her, when Grandma wasn't looking, putting more filling inside the triangles. I thought Grandma filled them just right: with music, love, and a heaping teaspoon each.

I loved the holidays and the parties: the feeling of anticipation as the guests arrived, the platters of food, the new clothes. One year my dad decided to surprise my mother for her birthday. My grandmothers put me and my sister into our never-yet-worn dresses, arranged food platters, and ushered in dozens of my mother's friends before my parents returned from a theater matinee. Everyone huddled in the dining room when we heard the car pull into the driveway. We heard footsteps. Dad's voice. Mom's voice. Dad opened the door and stepped aside to let Mom enter first. She caught sight of a few badly-hidden guests and shrieked, "Oh, no! Oh, no!" In her complete surprise, she thought perhaps she had invited all of those people over and forgotten about it!

My dad tried again only once, at a restaurant party for her fiftieth birthday. We all met in the city, and my grandmothers were walking in front of us towards the entrance. "Won't she be surprised to see all of her friends at the restaurant?" Grandma Rose said, in a loud whisper. Mom pretended not to have heard, pretended to have been surprised, and seemed to enjoy her party tremendously. Maybe Rose had wanted to soften Mom's surprise so she didn't yell "Oh, no!" at the guests.

For the restaurant party, I wore a blue three-quarter sleeve blouse and a flowered skirt. I had bought two similar outfits at the same time, but there were no more parties that season, and tags always stayed on clothes until an event was on the calendar. For years, I saved my best outfits for photo-worthy occasions or job interviews. Mom and I would look at the photos and remember the purchase, reminisce about the one or two times the outfit had been worn, and about how nice it had looked before it had become unfashionable, stained or outgrown.

Old habits die hard. One night in my early adulthood, I came home from work and dumped my keys and mail on the kitchen table, per usual. I changed into my favorite old jeans and faded sweatshirt, and hung my work clothes in the closet. Way in the back I noticed a blouse with the tags still on. The blouse had been there so long, I couldn't even remember when I had bought it. What a shame! I padded sockfooted through the apartment looking for my calendar, wondering whether I'd have a special occasion to wear the blouse before it went out of style. The calendar sat on the kitchen table under a growing pile of bills, magazines, and coupons. I would clear a corner later for my soda glass and eat with my crusty sandwich on a plate in my lap, watching the news.

Why would I do that? I remembered Gran's closet that had no clothes with tags on them, forbidden to be worn. I remembered the cleared dining table with the cloth napkins and utensils placed just so on the matching place mats. She had made me feel special. The party clothes had made me feel special. Why wasn't I special anymore?

I deliberately placed the calendar in a drawer, filed away all of the bills and other papers, and found my favorite woven place mats. I removed bread crust, made my sandwich, and cut it into triangles. Then I went to my closet, yanked the tags off that blouse, and wore it as I sat for dinner that night at my perfectly set table, just because I felt like it. I enjoyed that evening so much; I never ate with my plate on my lap again. I bought myself some pretty cloth napkins, and sometimes even poured my diet soda into a wine glass. It doesn't take much effort to make a simple meal special.

Gran passed before my children were born, but I know I am a better mother because of what she taught me. My kids rip tags off new clothes the second we get home. Though we don't always sit as a family for dinner, when we do, the table is cleared, and everyone feels important and loved.

I celebrate Gran's birthday with almost as much enthusiasm as if she were still on this earth, and always with new clothes and good food. One November 10, a group of friends and I met at a fine restaurant. A waitress overheard part of my annual speech and stopped to make conversation. "That's so sweet of you, toasting your grandmother. I hope that you will get to see her very soon."

"Oh, goodness, I hope not!" I replied a little too quickly. The waitress scuttled away with a look of horror, and I haven't been back to that place since.

The trick about losing grandparents is remembering that you were loved simply for existing, and that you'll always be worthy of such love. It must be different than losing a parent (knock-on-wood, I still have both of mine) because the role grandparents play is so different. Gran never disciplined me. She wasn't the one home worrying if I was five minutes past curfew. She was the one who, in my childish perspective, had no agenda or purpose in life other than to love me. I'm still the same person, still as worthy of her love, even though she isn't here anymore to speak the words. In my family, November 10 will always be a day of special food, special clothes, and special people. We remember her and honor her memory, and say the words she can no longer say.

Buffalo Wing Pizza

Grandma Sadie did not like growing old. "Never grow old," she once said to my husband, David. "It's no fun."

According to David, I was right there beside him when she said it, but I must have let the words fly by me without processing them. How could Grandma, who'd been to India and Japan, who'd gone on cruises and practiced yoga, who was the wisest and most loving person in the world, possibly feel old? But she did.

Maybe those words scared me because they implied she wasn't happy anymore, or perhaps they reminded me of her mortality. I couldn't imagine Grandma unhappy, nor could I imagine my life without her in it. I would try to make her happy as often as I could so that she would love being old and live forever.

I had seen real-life examples of people who lived long, happy, vibrant lives. My grandfather, Sadie's former husband, was a successful attorney and kept his mind active until he passed in his early nineties. He continued going in to his office, long after most people retire, not just to pretend to be busy and useful; he actually was busy and useful. Eventually he felt trapped in his aching, failing body and therefore ready to leave it, but that only happened at the very end.

I know another attorney (father of a friend of mine) who got a second hip replacement when he was eighty-four-years-old because his discomfort interfered with his golf game. Last I heard, he was ninety-two-years-old, still working and still swinging a club. What is it about lawyers and long lives? Frightening thought. Drew up some sort of contract with the afterlife, I suppose.

Of course Gran never told me how badly her arthritic knees bothered her or how many pills she took each day and what they were for. She wasn't one to complain. I had been free, therefore, to fool myself into thinking that "old age" meant nothing other than experience, wisdom, grace, and wrinkles.

To me, old was beautiful, and Gran was the old-age pin-up girl. "I earned every wrinkle," Gran would tell me. "I don't need to cover them up with makeup. I'm proud of them." She had gorgeous blue eyes, and the thickest pepper-and-salt hair I'd ever seen. I have pictures of her in her thirties and forties. While she was slimmer and snazzier then, wilder and more fashionable, she could never be more beautiful to me than she was with the wrinkles and no makeup.

After our wedding, David and I lived in Manhattan for three magical years. I loved the noise, the bustle, and even the smells of the city. You could be completely anonymous here, or create a village on your block by learning the first names of the local grocer, florist, and diner owner. Though David worked most weekends, I explored on my own. I spent hours in museums, enjoyed shows on Broadway and concerts at Lincoln Cen-

ter. Best of all, I had dinner with Gran at least one night each
week.

Every Tuesday my boss let me leave early to get to her
apartment, which was sixty blocks south and then east almost
until you hit the river. He probably thought I was such a good
kid, taking care of Grandma. How could I explain to him, or to
anyone, that I was being selfish? I was heading towards a person
who sat waiting just for me, who wanted to hear anything I had
to tell.

The doorman at Gran's building knew me, of course. He
let me in, and I'd stride confidently and excitedly through
the marble foyer to the elevator bay. I'd push the button for
the eighth floor and tap my foot impatiently as the elevator
climbed. I'd walk quickly down the long hallway, turn, continue to the end and stop in front of her door. My chest pound-
ed as if the person opening that door would tell me I'd won the
Super Lotto Jackpot, because that's just what it felt like every
Tuesday night.

Gran would greet me with a smile and a hug, and then
we'd sit a while. She asked me about my day, and I asked about
hers, and then came the usual: "Where would you like to eat
tonight? What are you in the mood for?" Even in Gran's quiet
neighborhood, there were many choices: Spanish, Polish, Chinese, Greek. We almost always chose the Chinese restaurant
across the street. The owner called out to us as we entered,
"Good evening, Grandma! Good evening, Grand-daughter!
Nice to see you! Come in, come in!"

Our usual waiter, named David like my husband, showed
us to our usual table. Grandma loved him. He was a young,

tall, gorgeous Chinese-American, and Grandma was a sucker for tall-dark-and-handsome. Grandma ordered the same meal every time: orange beef. "I'll have the steak, David," she'd say, touching his arm, "and some sake, please." David would wink and smile as he leaned down to take the menu from her. "Anything for you, Grandma!" he'd reply.

I remember well the first and only time Grandma traveled the sixty blocks and across town to see where I lived. I considered it an honor. She didn't take the subway, of course; she rode two buses and it took her almost an hour to reach us. For the first time, she didn't seem larger than life. I imagined her small and vulnerable in the crowded bus, in this huge city, outside the safety of her own neighborhood. David and I showed her around the apartment. "Everything is so new and bright!" she complimented. "What a gorgeous kitchen! This is lovely!"

Suddenly I felt embarrassed. Though her studio was spacious, I knew she missed having a separate bedroom. Though she felt at home where she lived, her apartment looked old and dated. At that moment, I wanted to switch apartments with her. David and I didn't really need our new kitchen; we ate out all the time. We didn't need a separate bedroom; we didn't entertain. It seemed unfair that this woman I worshipped lived in one weary room with an ancient kitchen while we spread out in this new and relatively luxurious apartment. Knowing Grandma, I'm sure she was genuinely happy for us, but even a saint would be entitled to a little jealousy? I couldn't wait to get outside. "Well, are you hungry? What are you in the mood for?"

We discussed options for dinner. "No, not Chinese. I have that in my neighborhood. Isn't there something different? I'd like to see where the young people go." Of course she did! For an evening, Grandma could be twenty-five with us. What a gift! We happily strolled arm-in-arm to The Firehouse, a converted firehouse bar/restaurant where the specialty was Buffalo Wing Pizza. We heard the din a block away. "Are you sure this will be okay, Grandma? It won't be too loud?" No, she would be thrilled to go there. "Okay then, let's go!"

The three of us shared a large Buffalo Wing Pizza, and we each drank a beer straight from the bottle. Grandma wanted the full experience, after all. She had the time of her life, taking in the crowd and even enjoying the spicy pizza. We stayed for hours, and finally convinced her it was time to go home. Though she insisted she could take the bus, we overpaid a cabbie and sent her home "in style."

After the Firehouse, Gran wanted more new experiences. First we decided to take her and my other grandmother, Rose, to the Royal Canadian Pancake House. It has closed since, but they had the absolute hugest pancakes on the planet, literally about 18 inches across, stacked five inches high, as well as other huge edibles. This was a real risk as far as planned outings go. Grandma Sadie tended to be up for anything, but Rose was finicky by nature. They peered questioningly at the sign above the door and entered in front of us, wondering what they had agreed to. As the hostess led us to our seats, my grandmothers' eyes grew wide looking at the portions served at the other tables. By the time they sat down, it was obvious they were flabbergasted.

"I've never seen such portions in my life!" Rose exclaimed.

"It's a week's worth on one plate!" agreed Sadie.

"I couldn't make a dent in those pancakes!" continued Rose.

"It's the craziest thing I've ever seen," agreed Sadie.

They locked eyes over their open menus and burst out laughing. "Isn't this fun?" they asked simultaneously (and rhetorically). They grinned throughout the meal, laughed like schoolgirls between bites, and each took home a very large, very full container of leftovers.

Sadie's next fun experience wasn't culinary—she hadn't been to the movies ("the pictures," she called them) in years. Disney's *Beauty and the Beast* had just come out, promising a new kind of animation, and she wanted to see it. The last time she had taken me to the movies, I was knee-high to a grasshopper, and *The Sound of Music* played at Radio City Music Hall. What a thrill! I had never been to such a place. I remember the grandeur, the crowd, the excitement, and Gran snoring through the show, her eyes closed behind her sunglasses.

Gran did not fall asleep during *Beauty and the Beast*. She tapped her fingers along with the music, gasped at the beauty of the Beast's library, shuddered at the townspeople who went to attack the castle. When Belle professed her love for the Beast, I thought I even saw a single tear roll down Gran's cheek. She remained alert and spellbound, and wouldn't leave until the last of the credits rolled by. "Oh," she exclaimed, "that was simply marvelous!"

"I loved it, too. Would you like to go to another movie sometime, Gran?"

"Oh, yes, dear, that would be wonderful!" she glowed.

"Hmmm...anything in particular you'd like to see?"

Looking at me innocently: "Well, that Tom Cruise fellow is awfully handsome."

My grandma, "old? " I think not!

Divorce: Water under the Bridge

Grandma Sadie's eyes spoke volumes of warmth, wisdom, and love. She had experienced painful things in her life including divorce at a time when it was a horrible embarrassment, but her eyes kept her secrets until I was an adult. "I didn't want to burden you, sweetie," she would say, though she didn't consider her past a burden at all. "Water under the bridge," she told me, "though it was difficult at the time. What's done is done."

In her day, people thought divorced women must have been dreadful to chase away their husbands, but no one dared discuss the subject. Better just to avoid the divorcees; it might be contagious! And of course, they might be eyeing your husband while your back is turned.

Divorce is so much more common today and doesn't carry the same stigma it used to. When my daughter was four, she made a love-list: a few boys to love now, one to marry, and another to marry when she was done with the first marriage. I hadn't imagined that her preschool friends could expose her to so much of real life; I certainly hope it wasn't in the curriculum!

Many of our friends married within a few years of David and me, and we were all confident that statistics would not apply to our circle. The most beautiful wedding we attended was actually the smallest. Mike and Carol married in a country church as tiny as a playhouse and white as fresh-fallen snow. They held their reception in a hundred-year-old inn with wide-plank floors and bright windows open to a rich, green spring: tradition and new birth, side by side, wrapped up with a satin bow. I cried at that wedding, certain that such a magnificent beginning must be the sign of many happy years to come.

We spent a lot of time with that lucky couple before they moved out of state two years later. They promised to invite us down to see their new, three-bedroom dream house, just as soon as they had finished painting and refurnishing it. But by then Mike's girlfriend and her three children had moved in, and Carol had bought herself the tiniest two-room cottage I could imagine (our first apartment had been bigger). She was devastated. She'd lost everything in one agonizing cut of the knife: her husband, her lovely home, her hopes for starting a family.

I hopped on a plane to make sure she was OK. She was fine, but barely recognizable. Gone were the pearls and sweater sets. Now it was all tight jeans and low-cut blouses, leather boots and heavy lipstick. She'd bought herself a shiny, red sports car and some Jimmy Buffet CDs.

We went out to a bar one night to meet up with some of her new single friends. "You're not actually going to wear that out in public?" she chastised as we prepared to leave her house. "You look like, oh, I don't know, some happy homemaker from the 1950s!" Well, that was how I felt, and that was all I had brought to wear. I didn't own tight blue jeans or a low-cut black blouse, and certainly would not have looked as good in that outfit as she did. Carol was a Young Turk out on the town, and I looked like her chaperone.

The bar experience felt like college all over again. Carol ran into a guy she'd been virtually stalking for weeks, but left with the phone number of his more willing friend. I skulked in a corner, as usual, with my Diet Coke, and melted into the wall; she almost left without me. The next day we headed for the mall to get matching second piercings in our left ears, as symbols of sisterhood and rebellion during her period of renewal. Her piercing was quick and easy. Mine hurt like hell, got infected, and eventually had to close over. She was ready for a second. The body that could squeeze into those tight jeans could certainly handle a second hole. The chubby chaperone body would only reject it.

On the plane ride home, I took a Tylenol and tried to ignore my throbbing earlobe. I opened my wallet and pulled out David's picture. Yup, still butterflies. I was happy not to have the need for a low-cut blouse or a second hole in my ear.

But that was the 1990s, and Gran got divorced long before that. I don't know exactly when, but she had already been divorced for a while when my parents married in 1964. It was quite the scandal for mom to marry into one of "those families." Even now, many divorced women find themselves shut out of activities with their married friends. I imagine Grandma had to remake herself, though not the way Carol did. I couldn't imagine Gran in a red convertible, blasting "Margaritaville" on the CD player, and picking up guys in a bar.

My mother adored Sadie, her mother-in-law. She always stood up for her, told me how Sadie had been wronged by her husband who left her for a young, blonde secretary. Grandma, however, never said anything bad about her ex-husband or his second wife. She explained that sometimes things work out, but sometimes they don't. She wished him all the best. "Water under the bridge."

Of course, children don't always get the whole truth. One part of the story I never heard until I was an adult is how Grandma sowed her wild oats after the divorce, not as unlike Carol as I had thought! When my mother told me about it, she was probably torn between cautioning me against such shocking behavior and shouting "Good for her!" at the top of her lungs. Unfortunately, now that I am old enough and mature enough to hear the story from the horse's mouth, Grandma isn't here to tell it.

The fact is, many truths can probably describe her history and all be true. I accept that Grandma wasn't perfect. No one really is; no families are. My daughter once said, "Mommy, I'm grateful for my brother." I told her that was sweet, that I was grateful for her brother, too. "No, Mommy, you don't understand! See, without brother, our family would be perfect. But only G-d can be perfect, so that wouldn't be right; so I'm grateful for my brother."

What is perfect, anyway? Would staying married have made Grandma's picture less imperfect? Their marriage was unhappy. He was unfaithful. They were not a good match. He was happier with the blonde secretary, and stayed with her faithfully and devotedly until his death at ninety-something.

Here's another fact: my grandmother had a serious love affair after the divorce. This, too, I didn't know until it was too late. Until well after "Grandpa" Jack died, that is. I thought he was just one of her friends, like "Grandma" Faye, close enough for a term of endearment but not to be an actual family member. "What a nice man," Grandma would say about him.

Judging from old photographs, Jack may have entered Grandma's life when I was four or five. His wife had refused to give him a divorce but moved herself to Florida, where she lived happily in a senior's community and made holiday calls to him and their grown children in New York. Again, it was a different time; people accepted and understood the situation, and she avoided the divorce stigma. In fact, even Jack's children understood. Seeing their father so lonely, it was actually his children who introduced him to Sadie, his soul mate and partner until the day he died.

I only understood the depth of Gran's loss many years later. At the time of Jack's passing, I was too young to comprehend the loss anyway, and when I was old enough, people supposed there was no point in telling me. Finally Gran told me herself, and I wondered if she had mourned alone, supposed that his family mourned with his legal wife and not his true love, and doubted that Grandma had received the support she needed.

The problem with protecting people from "unattractive" truths is that the ignorant cannot make their own judgment as to whether that truth is unattractive at all. Certainly it seems far more unattractive to me that she may have mourned alone than that Jack technically was married to another woman. How could I possibly judge a woman who never once judged me? The woman who wished her wealthy husband all the best, with his lavish lifestyle, multiple homes, and sexy wife, while she lived frugally in a one-room apartment? Regardless of our opinions, shouldn't we all have been there to hold her?

"I'm so sorry, Grandma. I didn't know what he was to you."

"It's OK, dear. You were just a child; you didn't know."
More water under the bridge.

A Pretty Girl

To my mother, my Grandma Rose was everything a woman should be: loving and charismatic, personable and quick to laugh. She dressed well, cooked well, and performed good deeds all around the neighborhood. But when Mom had a solo in her school's spring concert, Rose couldn't leave the office to attend. No one waved to Mom from the audience, or clapped louder than all the others and shouted her name.

Grandma Rose had blue eyes hidden behind thick glasses, and blonde hair always styled just-so and protected by an impenetrable layer of hairspray. She loved looking pretty, and loved looking at pretty things. But I also remember her being sticky. When she kissed me, she left a sticky red lipstick mark on my cheek. Her car seats had sticky protective covers on them. At one point she had plastic slipcovers all over her furniture and even on the path of carpet that led to the couch. I thought maybe her hair had a slipcover on it, too.

"A pretty girl is like a melody," she would croon as I showed off a new outfit. She loved new outfits, too. Mom used to shop for her. The Grandmas, as we called Rose and Sadie collectively, would arrive together on a weekend morning to see the grandkids and receive armloads of clothing Mom had bought at a nearby shop for mature women. After they oohed and aahed and hugged and kissed Diana and me, we would sit and watch them go through all of the outfits: pantsuits for Rose, tops-and-skirts for Sadie. They were always color-coordinated, just like the Danskin play clothes Diana and I wore. It all made sense to us: people who liked to play had to have clothes that match easily.

"Let me look at you," Rose would say as she walked in the door. When I was little, that was fine. I'd do my famous model imitation, complete with a turn and a snap of the head. "Aren't you beautiful!" she would predictably cry. As an awkward pre-teen, it made me nervous. "That's my little lady!" After my first child arrived, it made me ashamed. "You could lose a few pounds," she'd remind me. Good thing she can't see me now; she'd have a field day. Sometimes I could swear it's her voice I hear in my head saying, "Mitts off! Those cookies are for the children!"

Rose used to bake cookies, dozens and dozens of wonderful, scrumptious cookies. She was famous for them. My favorites were called Russian Wedding Balls: butter-cookie flavor but round like tiny globes, and rolled in powdered sugar to represent the sweetness of a new marriage. They had crushed nuts inside but the outside was always smooth and perfect. The outside had to be perfect, you see, and the bumps were hidden deep underneath the surface. That was life.

Grandma Rose grew up in a time when people didn't talk about nuts or bumps. Her family had both. We heard plenty of stories about Iris, her sister, but only the powdered sugar stories. "Oh, what a beauty Iris was." "The boys always flocked around Iris." As an adult, I learned that Iris was an agoraphobic, sitting around her house with the air conditioning blasting and wearing a fur coat because, well, she had to have one, and it was winter outside. In Grandma's defense, I have seen pictures of Iris and agree that she was movie-star gorgeous. It must have been hard for Rose to grow up in her shadow; but she was, in fact, a nut.

So Iris was the nut, and sadly, there was also a bump: her son, my Uncle George. George was an Rh baby, born with so many problems it was a miracle he survived. He was never healthy, never really whole, and it broke Grandma's heart. If he had been born today, his life would have been completely different, but the doctor who replaced the one who went off to war did not take the necessary precautions. Poor George had a sweet, gentle soul. He loved and relied on his mother, and he positively adored my mother, his "shining star" of a big sister. She could do no wrong in his eyes, and was often left in charge of him while my grandmother went to work.

There weren't many choices at the time, so Rose took a job as a secretary. It must have been a wonderful distraction to her troubles at home, working with things that she could control and helping people with problems she could fix. Given her love for fashion, I imagine she dressed stylishly, matching her handbags and heels to each outfit, keeping her hair and nails perfect. But she was also extremely intelligent and competent. In time, she became assistant editor of the entire trade magazine.

So Grandma Rose had become a pioneer among women, and an inspiration to many. Her success, however, could not cure her son's illness or prevent her husband from dying suddenly of a heart attack. Her success with powdered sugar only covered the bumps for those who never got close enough to sample the cookies, nor could her success ever make her as pretty as Iris. Looking back, I have more patience for the "pretty girl" song. Powdered sugar and powdered makeup aren't that different. When life is tough and the landscape looks bleak, you do what you can to make it look better.

During Rose's last years, though she was wheelchair bound, and suffered from dizzy spells and heart problems, she was happy as a clam. Why? She was down to 121 pounds. "Aren't I beautiful?" she would crow. Yes, but not for that reason, Grandma. Not for that reason.

Fairy-Tale Love

The year I turned eight, Grandma Rose got married. I remember the year because it was the same year my parents took in an exchange student from the Philippines, and also the year that Sadie took me on the 747 to California. This was the year I learned to accept unfamiliar people into my family: a foreign student, a cranky great-uncle, and a brand-new grandfather.

Rose became a widow before my second birthday. I don't remember Grandpa Ira, but I have a single photograph of him holding me in his lap, both of us looking at the camera. I love him, just from that picture. The few stories I heard of him were all glowing and filled with admiration. He was a quiet, thoughtful man who worked hard at the family lumber yard, adored his family, and played the saw or the violin while my mom accompanied him on the piano. Ira's brothers and their children all lived on the same block, and the cousins ran freely between houses. Then Ira died, and Grandma's world fell apart.

Seven years later, a miracle happened. A friend introduced her to a kind, slightly older gentleman who was also alone. Rose became a school girl once again. She had light in her eyes as she looked at him, a shy smile, and obvious delight in his company. They went out to dinner, took walks in the park, and courted in the old-fashioned way with flowers delivered, doors opened, and compliments paid. A retired lighting salesman became, for her, a knight in shining armor. Charlie introduced her to his family, and she introduced him to us. Eventually, he asked my mother's permission to propose to Rose. The ceremony took place in my parent's living room.

My family accepted Charlie immediately and completely. Only now do I fully appreciate the significance of the entire course of events, from its storybook beginning to what remains, to this day, one of the most romantic weddings I have ever attended. I distinctly remember wearing a new dress, strutting proudly and importantly among the guests, and looking up all the time because the house was full of grown-ups. I remember Grandma's dress, too, and how pretty she looked. Mostly I remember Grandma's constant smile, and the pink glow in her cheeks as she giggled and blushed throughout the reception. Charlie quietly watched her as she moved with joyful luminescence as the center of attention. He only had eyes for her, and she adored him.

At eight years of age, I fell in love for the first time, with weddings. My own daughter has yet to attend a wedding, but she started playing "bride" as early as age three. She would put on her prettiest dress, her daddy would wear a tie, and they would promise to love each other. "Say I do, Daddy! Then I say I do, too!" The game became more complex as she got older. Someone would have to hum the wedding march. That person would also officiate. After the bride and groom exchanged their vows, they danced around the living room. When the festivities were over, the groom got a big hug. "The wedding is over now, Daddy! Give me your credit card so I can go to the mall."

Belief in fairy tale endings is no longer fashionable because so few people get them, not because women don't want them. The iPods of the world play love songs as much as Victrolas did in the old days; modern movies include as many romances as did the old black-and-whites, only now sex is artfully imitated rather than implied. Expectations for getting what we want have increased in almost every way: equal pay, challenging job opportunities, larger homes, helpful appliances and gadgets, two-minute drive-throughs and ninety-second speed-dating. It's no wonder the fairy tale ending has become unattainable; it's been completely redefined.

Many women I know claim they need a wife, not a husband. They tire of expectations reaching in all directions at once, of being a bread-winner, housewife, mother, and Saturday night sex siren while their men come home and turn on the football game. In the old days, women stayed home, and if they complained, it was quietly and cautiously. Even today, however, once a couple has reached a twenty-year anniversary, the assumption is that they will remain a couple, no matter how cordial or turbulent, symbiotic or dysfunctional the relationship has become. These are people who have grown to know every habit, every story, every found-again childhood chum of their partners, and who expect to grow old together. They don't always get to. Rose didn't get her chance.

Rose lost Ira, and then she lost Charlie thirteen years after she said "I do." I cannot fathom the pain of being twice widowed, but I am almost certain that if she had the opportunity, she would have married again. If even at the age of ninety, a handsome wheelchair-bound gentleman had commented on the sparkle of her eyes or the music of her laughter, she would once again risk a broken heart. A heart that would not love had no place in her life.

If she were alive today and a great deal younger, people would no doubt caution her or even laugh behind her back. With divorce reaching an all-time high, women who think Prince Charming exists are often ridiculed. Even if you are deeply in love at your wedding, years later you could be bitterly disappointed, or left penniless and pregnant. You're a princess for a day, but as soon as your rear-end starts to sag, your prince may be looking for a replacement. "Little girls, burn those wedding dress-ups and plastic tiaras, because that just ain't the way life is!" Still, we don't tell them that. We let them play bride because we know deep down, we wish it were possible for all of us to make that dream a reality.

If only you could have seen the way Rose looked at Charlie! When I saw that look, I knew that's what I wanted to have some day. I'm not foolish enough to believe that wanting that kind of love is enough to get it, or even to overlook that mature love may be more sensible and patient than young love. I've met women who love their husbands but can't see them through another rehab or stint in jail, and women whose husbands walked out without explanation or who were dangerous to their children.

All I'm saying is, when I was eight-years-old, Grandma Rose showed me that love can happen at any age, with wrinkles and on a fixed income, without a long, white dress or a fancy party with a band. Love can happen to someone who has dealt with a life as often tough and unforgiving as it was generous and joyful. It happened for her in part because she refused to give up on it. As far as I'm concerned, Caitlin can play bride dress-up as much as she wants. She may never meet her Charlie—but then again, she just might.

Made in the USA
Charleston, SC
25 January 2013